The Crucible of Europe
The ninth and tenth centuries
in European history

GEOFFREY BARRACLOUGH

The Crucible of Europe

The ninth and tenth centuries
in European history

with 61 black and white illustrations

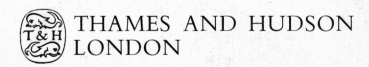
THAMES AND HUDSON
LONDON

1 *Frontispiece* An eleventh-century impression of the
geography of Europe; detail of a world map from a French
manuscript

Printed and bound in Great Britain by Jarrold and Sons Ltd Norwich

Contents

Preface

EVEN in the post-European age in which we live, the making of Europe is a fascinating story, a perennial source of interest and stimulus. This book is concerned with one of its more obscure and neglected chapters. The ninth and tenth centuries – the period with which it largely deals – get short shrift in most general histories. By comparison with the preceding and succeeding ages, they were dim, and grim, and dark; and the temptation to pass them by as quickly as possible, to jump from the 'great' age of Charlemagne to the flowering of medieval civilization in the days of St Bernard and St Francis, is understandable enough. To do so would be to misunderstand the way things happen. The ninth and tenth centuries were a formative period in European history, every bit as much as the better known periods which preceded and succeeded them, and it was out of the anarchy and tribulation which men and women of that generation suffered that a new Europe took shape.

How and why this transformation occurred, how a new Europe was born out of the old Europe which had arisen on the soil of the Roman empire, is the subject-matter of this book. That means that it is concerned primarily with political and what used to be called constitutional history. Some readers, I suspect, may find this a distinctly old-fashioned approach. During the past thirty or forty years, the tendency among historians has been to turn away from political history in the direction of intellectual history, ideas and the climate of thought. This is a tendency with which I have every sympathy. Few things could be more sterile than lists of kings and dates of battles a thousand years ago. Nevertheless, the ninth century, at least in its latter half, was not noteworthy for creative intellectual activity; and such developments of lasting significance as there were, took place in the sphere of government and institutions. Institutional history may be less important at some epochs than at others, but in the period with which this book deals, it seems to me that the emergence, out of the Carolingian inheritance, of the different institutions of the different European peoples – institutions which left a lasting imprint on their subsequent history – is the essence of the story.

Finally, it should be said that this book deals almost exclusively with the successor states of the Carolingian empire – that is to say, with (or with the lands which were to become) France, Germany, and Italy. I have included a chapter on Anglo-Saxon England, because the comparison between the British Isles and the Continent is instructive; and I have made some mention – probably a good deal less than I should – of the states of eastern and northern Europe, where they enter the scene. I have entirely excluded Byzantium and the Balkans, and after some hesitation I have omitted Spain which, until the very end of the period, was almost entirely under Islamic rule. These limitations are probably hard to justify, but anything else would have required a different and far longer book. Those who desire a broader picture will find in the bibliography at the end a number of titles which remedy the defect.

G. B.

One
Prelude to Charlemagne: the Frankish ascendancy

THE MAKING OF EUROPE is a long, complicated and hesitant process. The idea of Europe as a distinctive unity gradually took shape in the Middle Ages, but it was not until the turn of the seventeenth and eighteenth centuries that it emerged as the unchallenged symbol of a larger human loyalty.[1] Down to the close of the fifteenth century the countries of Europe were still on the fringe of the civilized world, outstripped by China, by far the most civilized and powerful state in the world at the time, and threatened and hemmed in by the great, expanding Muslim empire of the Ottoman Turks. The major shift in the focus of world history, which made Europe the chief centre of power and civilization for upward of two centuries from 1750 to 1950, only came towards the end of the seventeenth century, when the Ottoman thrust was halted and reversed, and when at the same time the movement of expansion, conquest and settlement in Asia and the Americas, which had begun sporadically in the sixteenth century, began to make headway.

Europe, in any but a purely geographical sense, is a product of its history. The Roman empire was a Mediterranean empire, straddling three continents. Even after the conquest of Gaul and Britain, the northern provinces towards the Rhine and Danube were little more than military colonies, outposts of empire occupied to hold off the barbarians beyond the pale, and the Mediterranean remained the axis of the Roman world, even after the fabric of Roman hegemony began to crumble. Medieval history, in its broadest connotation, is the story of the way the axis of history shifted from the Mediterranean to the lands north of the Alps, of the destruction of the Roman equilibrium, the severance of the regions held together by Rome, and the rise of a distinctive European civilization.

THE WESTERN ROMAN EMPIRE EXTINGUISHED

Two far-ranging movements of peoples destroyed the equilibrium of the ancient world. The first was the influx, across the Danube and the Rhine, of Germanic and Slav invaders; the second the rise and expansion of Islam. Of the two, it was the second which fractured for all time the framework of Mediterranean civilization. The early Germanic kingdoms of the fifth and sixth centuries – the Ostrogoths in Italy, the Visigoths in Spain, the Burgundians and Franks in Gaul – had clung as far as possible to

9

their Roman inheritance, interested only in exploiting it and profiting from it. The advance of Islam in the seventh century, cutting the sea-routes in the Mediterranean, and isolating the northern shores of the Mediterranean from Africa and Asia Minor, had far more drastic results. At the same time, the descent of the Slavs into the Balkan peninsula and of the Lombards into Italy severed the land-routes between the surviving Roman empire in Constantinople and the west, and cut off the western barbarians from the centres of civilization.

The results were catastrophic. If the sixth century had seen at least partial recovery from the disruption of the fifth century, the seventh century, particularly the period from 640 to 718, was a time of dislocation, crisis and a real break in continuity.[2] Commerce shrank to nothing, Greek and Syrian merchants disappeared from the cities of Gaul and Spain, and agriculture became the mainstay of the economy. The results were fatal to the surviving Germanic kingdoms in the west. The drift to the land had begun much earlier, as a result of the severe economic crisis which overtook the Roman empire in the third century; but now the western territories became a society of landlords and peasants, of villages and estates, organized largely for subsistence. The ruling dynasties were also impoverished and weakened. Lacking liquid capital, they were no longer able to maintain a salaried administration, relying instead on their household servants and retainers, and travelling from estate to estate with their retinues, exactly like other great landed noblemen, eating up the produce and collecting their dues and rents.

THE RISE OF THE FRANKS

The most successful of the barbarian kingdoms had been that of the so-called Salian Franks, who swept down in the fifth century from the region between the Meuse and the Rhine and occupied northern Gaul as far as the river Loire. The creation of the Frankish kingdom was the work of Clovis (482–511), the founder of the Merovingian dynasty, who united the Frankish warrior bands, embraced the Christian faith, and established his rule over both the Frankish invaders and the surviving Gallo-Roman population. The success of the Franks under Clovis and his successors was prodigious. The Visigoths who had occupied south-western France were driven south of the Pyrenees in 507. In 531 Thuringia in the east was conquered, three years later it was the turn of the kingdom of Burgundy, in 537 Provence in the south was acquired with the Mediterranean ports of Marseilles and Toulon, and in the same year the Alemannian lands in south-west Germany and modern Switzerland. When Bavaria was brought into dependence in 539, the Frankish dominion extended over the whole area formerly ruled by Rome in western Europe north of the Alps and Pyrenees.

But the Frankish success was as ephemeral as it was rapid. No doubt the very speed of the advance overtaxed Frankish resources. Moreover, the Salians were too few in numbers to maintain their hegemony, and, having moved away from their homeland north of the Rhine in a great

2 The baptism of Clovis by St Rémy; from a ninth-century ivory carving

encircling movement, they quickly lost touch and were absorbed into the Gallo-Roman nobility with which they intermarried. Already as early as 561 the kingdom was divided into three parts, and in 614 the division was made definite. One part was the old kingdom of the Burgundians, which thus retained something of its identity; the second was Neustria, or the new land in the west, which the Salian Franks had conquered and occupied; and the third was Austrasia, or the eastern territory on both sides of the Rhine, which was settled by Frankish tribes known (because they lived on the banks of the river) as Ripuarians, who had been brought under Salian rule at an early date.

After 614 the relationship between the Salians and the Ripuarians was reversed and Austrasia gradually asserted its predominance, as the Merovingian dynasty founded by Clovis, weakened by lavish grants of estates and properties to the church and to nobles, lost its hold. Each of the three regions now had its own mayor of the palace, who was the effective ruler, the first mayor in Austrasia being Pippin the Elder, the founder of the Carolingian dynasty. The rise of the Carolingians transformed the whole situation. The kingdom of the Salian Franks was no more viable than the other early barbarian kingdoms, and by 639, when it had used up its inherited wealth, it was on the edge of bankruptcy. But now another Frankish people, the Ripuarians, took over under the Carolingian dynasty, and gradually restored order. The turning-point came in 687 at the battle of Tertry, when Pippin II defeated the Neustrians and became mayor of the palace for the whole kingdom. The unity of the Frankish kingdom was maintained, but after 687 the centre of gravity shifted decisively from Neustria to the Ripuarian lands in the region of the Meuse, the Moselle and the lower Rhine.

11

3 St Boniface, 'apostle of the Germans', began to christianize the Germans in 715 at the behest of pope Gregory II; his martyrdom in 754 is the subject of this tenth-century miniature

There is no need to describe the stages by which, after 687, the Carolingians halted the decline, consolidated their position, and then went over to the offensive. The process was slow and little was permanently achieved until Charles Martel succeeded his father, Pippin II, in 714. The first necessity was to ensure control in Neustria, and this was done by what has sometimes been called a 'secularization' of church lands. In reality the churches, which were by now the greatest landowners, were compelled to grant or lease out estates to Charles's nominees, the result being that he now had a body of devoted and reliable vassals – the so-called *vassi dominici* – spread out far and wide through the Frankish lands, men who would obey his orders and carry out his commands. Equally important was the reform and reorganization of the thoroughly secularized Frankish church, which was carried out with the help of the great Anglo-Saxon missionary, St Boniface. In this way was formed the alliance between the Carolingians and the church, which contributed so much to the strength and prestige of the Frankish monarchy in the second half of the eighth century. It was Boniface who anointed Charles Martel's son, Pippin III, with oil, when it was decided in 751 to dethrone the last shadowy Merovingian king and set the Carolingian in his place; and the new king's authority as 'the Lord's anointed' won him and his successors the active support of the leaders of the Frankish church.

Secure at home, the new dynasty was able to embark on conquest abroad. The first task, largely accomplished by the time of the death of Charles Martel in 741, was to restore Frankish control in Thuringia and Alemannia as it had been in 539, before the onset of Merovingian anarchy. Bavaria also was brought into dependence again, though its subjugation had to be repeated in 788. Nevertheless by 754, when

Pippin intervened in Italy against the Lombard king at the request of pope Stephen II, the foundations were laid for the Carolingian empire of Charles the Great. Born in 742 and succeeding to the throne (at first jointly with his brother) in 768, Charles carried on the expansion his father and grandfather had begun. First, he turned to the conquest of the heathen Saxons, the only remaining German tribe outside the Frankish orbit, a task which occupied him, off and on, for thirty years. In 773 the Saxon wars were broken off to cope with Lombardy, conquered and brought under Charles's rule after a quick campaign in 774. In 775 he was back in Saxony, which resisted fiercely in spite of bitter repression, only to switch in 778 to Spain, where he suffered defeat.

Nothing is more characteristic of Charles than his restless energy, as he switches from one frontier to another, always thrusting forward: back to Saxony from 782 to 785, in 791 against the Avars on the Danube, in 795 in Spain to guard the southern flank by forming the Spanish March round Barcelona. In 796 there follows a further campaign against the Avars, which brings rich booty, the setting up of the Bavarian Ostmark, and the establishment of the archbishopric of Salzburg as a centre for the missionizing of the newly conquered heathen land. In 799 Charles is back in Paderborn, conducting operations against the rebellious Saxons. In 800 he goes to Italy for a campaign against the Byzantine forces south of Rome, and is crowned emperor by the pope in St Peter's. But expansion and conquest go on after 800 as before, though Charles never again returns to Italy. In 804 there is a last successful campaign against the Saxons, followed immediately by an attack on the Slav peoples, the Sorbs and Obodrites, on the eastern boundary of Saxony. In 805 and 806 there are expeditions to Bohemia, which is made tributary.

It is a tale of vast, restless energy, of a people borne along on the crest of a wave of expansion, even more remarkable than that of the Salian Franks between 507 and 539. By the end of Charles's reign most of continental Europe west of the Elbe had been united under Frankish rule. The Frankish boundaries had been expanded into Spain, to the river Elbe in the east, north to the Baltic Sea, and south beyond Rome (though not to include the whole of Italy). Not surprisingly, most historians have seen the establishment of the Carolingian empire as 'the central feature' of European history between the fall of the Roman empire in the west and the emergence of the feudal monarchies in the thirteenth century.[3]

A FRANKISH EUROPE

What can be said without fear of contradiction is that by 800 the long period of transition, beginning with Diocletian and Constantine four centuries earlier, was over in the west. Something like a European civilization, still primitive but with definite characteristics of its own, was coming into existence. Outside Byzantium – and even there the innovations put through by Heraclius and the Isaurian emperors had wrought great and lasting changes – the last vestiges of the ancient world had disappeared. The supersession of the Merovingian by the Carolingian

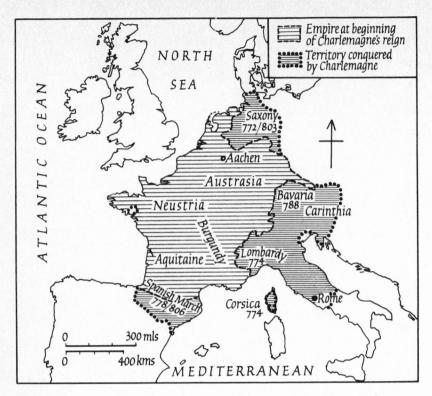

4 The lands which Charlemagne inherited and those he added to his empire by conquest

dynasty meant the abandoning of the last shaky Roman elements in government. It also meant the displacement of a civilization centred round the trade routes of the Mediterranean basin by a landlocked continental civilization with its axis in the Austrasian lands between the Rhine, the Meuse and the Moselle.[4] Down to the end of the sixth century, the important provinces of the west had been those bordering on the Mediterranean. When Spain was lost to Islam, and Italy, ruined by the long Gothic wars, was occupied by the Lombards, the centre of gravity moved northwards from the shores of the Mediterranean, which had suddenly become hostile and menacing, and western Europe was reduced to living on its own meagre resources. The result, inevitably, was the emergence of a new economic and social order, based on land, and the wealth accruing from land.

The contrast between the Merovingian and the Carolingian ages is too manifest to be gainsaid. Nevertheless, it would be a mistake to exaggerate the magnitude of the change. It used to be almost axiomatic that the Carolingian empire was the foundation of medieval – and, indeed, of modern – Europe, the 'starting-point of the whole development of western civilization'.[5] In reality, though the break with the past was real,

14

the situation was still inchoate and in constant flux. Far from being the hinge between two worlds, the Carolingian empire was really a temporary halting-place; and it has rightly been pointed out that, if the division of Charles the Great's empire in 806 had been carried out, the future shape of Europe would have been entirely different from that which actually came to pass.[6] In many ways, the Carolingian empire was an end rather than a beginning, or at least it partook – as most societies do – of both aspects: that is to say, it looked back and it looked forward, and if it was modern by comparison with the past, it was old-fashioned by comparison with the future. The very attempt to impose a statute upon Europe, to weld the whole continent into a single political and cultural unit, was more reminiscent of Rome than of the Europe of different peoples and different nations to which the future was reserved.

There is, therefore, some truth in the view that the real starting-point of European history was not the empire pieced together by the Franks in the eighth century, but the emergence, in the ninth and tenth centuries, of states springing up on Carolingian soil, but built upon other foundations. A hundred years after Charlemagne's death, the picture was totally different, the structure permanently and irretrievably altered. But such questions are more a matter of words than of facts. No one will deny the importance of the Carolingian inheritance; but, if we wish to understand how it contributed to the shaping of Europe, we must see it as it was, with all its defects and limitations, as well as its positive achievements. If, as has been said, Carolingian Europe was the foundation and starting-point of the future development of western civilization, it was as much because of its failures as because of its successes.

5 Left, statue of Charles the Great (742–814), dated *c.* 900

6 The silver denier (above), issued during the last ten years of Charles's reign, shows him with the olive leaves of a Roman emperor

7 Right above, eagle motif from the so-called 'Mantle of Charlemagne'

8 Right below, a Roman sarcophagus of the late second century which was said to have been Charles's tomb

Two   The Carolingian legacy

THE FRANKISH EMPIRE was only a very small part of Europe physically, and it is important to realize its limits. It extended eastward only as far as the river Elbe, as far as the mountains of Bohemia and the Alpine districts of Austria, where Charles the Great, after defeating the Avars, set up an outpost with its centre in Salzburg. It extended southwards only as far as the Arab outposts in the Pyrenees, and the Byzantine outposts in the far south of Italy, which remained Greek-speaking territory. Northern Europe, Scandinavia and Denmark, was still heathen and remained heathen until the eleventh century. Efforts were made after 820 at cultural contacts through missionaries; the foundation of the archbishopric of Hamburg in 831 was intended to establish a missionary centre for the work, in much the same way as the foundation of Mainz in 751 had provided the keystone of the German mission. St Ansgar, first archbishop of Hamburg, 'the apostle of the north', is often compared with St Boniface. But he was much less successful than his predecessor, mainly, perhaps, because the ninth-century Carolingians were unable, as Charles Martel had done in the case of Boniface and Charles the Great did in the case of the Saxon mission, to give him the backing of the sword; and so the north, even Denmark, remained outside the orbit of Carolingian civilization. So also did England, which was still contributing to the education of Frankish society through churchmen such as Alcuin of York, rather than absorbing Frankish influences. Relations between Offa of Mercia and Charles the Great were close and friendly; but it would not be true to say that England was a part of Carolingian Europe.

This 'Europe', therefore, was very small. It did not even comprise all the areas of Germanic settlement, and it was hemmed in not only by the great empires of Islam and Rome, both far ahead in civilization, but also by a solidly Slav bloc east of the Elbe. Nor, of course, did it comprise the whole extent of Latin Christendom: not only Anglo-Saxon England, but also the small remaining Christian communities in the north of Spain remained outside the Frankish sphere – the latter definitely hostile and prepared to fight with the Moors against the Franks, when need arose.[1] We must, therefore, beware of exaggerations which would see in Charles the Great and the Frankish empire, which he instituted, the representatives either of western Christendom, or of Europe, or even of

18

9 Alcuin's version of the Vulgate, illustrating the 'Carolingian minuscule' script which replaced the Anglo-Saxon style (see p. 26)

INCPT REGV
LIBER PRIMVS

FVIT VIR fr
unus dera
mathaimso
phim demon
te ephraim
et nomen ei
elchana fi
lius hiero
boam filii heliu filii thau
filii suph ephrateus et habu
it duas uxores nomen unian
na et nomen secundae fen
nena fuerunt q̃ fennenae
filii annae autem non eran
liberi et ascendebat ir ille
de ciuitate sua statutis die
bus ut adoraret et sacrificaret dño exer
cituu insilo Erant autem ibi duo filii
heli ofni et finees sacerdotes dñi uenit
ergo dies et immolauit helchana deditq; fen
nenae uxori suae et cunctis filiis eius et filiab;
partes Annae autem dedit partem unam tristis
quia annam diligebat Dñs autem concluserat
uuluam eius affligebat quoq; eam aemula eius
et uehementer angebat intantum ut exprobra
ret quod conclusisset dñs uuluam eius sicq; faciebat
per singulos annos Cum redeunte tempore ascende
rent templum dñi et sic prouocabat eam Porro illa
flebat et non capiebat cibum Dixit ergo ei helcha
na uir suus Anna cur fles et quare non comedes et
quam obrem affligitur cor tuum numquid non ego
melior sum tibi quam decem filii Surrexit autem
anna postquam comederat insilo et biberat et heli
sacerdote sedente super sellam ante postes templi
dñi Cum esset anna amaro animo orauit dñm flens
largiter et uotum uouit dicens Dñe exercituum si
respiciens uideris afflicationem famulae tuae et
recordatus mei fueris nec oblitus ancillae tuae

qomades Re
quit domine m
ego iinumq;
bibi sed effudi
Nereputes anc
lial quia ex m
locutasum usq;
cce tristicir det
dixit Ut anam
oculis tuis Et
uultusq; illius
Et surrexerun
reuersiq; sue
tha Cognouit
suam et recor
circulum dier
uocauit q; nom
see eu Ascendit
immolarent d
anna non asce
donec ablacte
ante conspectu
et helchana uir
et mane donec
uerbum suum
lium suu donec
eum secum po
trib; modiis fa
addomum dñi
tulus et imm
rum heli Et a
mat ua domine
ram et hi cora
michi dñs peti
Idcirco et ego
quib; fuerit a
ibi dñm Et
EXVLTAV
tum e cor meu
super inimico
non est fidei
e foras sicut

Germanic Europe. All his dominions represent is the force of Frankish arms, the conquests of a warrior people, which used its new powers of organization to subject its neighbours. But within the area of Frankish control Europe did, in the century roughly between 750 and 850, take on a Frankish imprint, or (perhaps more correctly) was forced into a Frankish mould. It was, as we shall see, a very rough process, enforced by harsh means, which was not in the long run nearly so successful as is often supposed. From the middle of the ninth century, the Frankish veneer wore thin, the Frankish mould began to crack, and the underlying differences again came to light. But for about a century a rough-and-ready uniformity was imposed; and this was one factor – though not the only factor – in the making of the future.

It led, in the first place, to a basic similarity of institutions. It led also, so far as we can speak of civilization, to a basic similarity of civilization, so that where in the previous period each region had gone its own way, now the only civilization left on the continent of Europe, outside the spheres of Islam and of Byzantium, was Carolingian. It meant that there was one ruling class with a basically similar outlook and basically similar interests throughout a wide area covering Gaul and Germany and Italy; and it led to a similar uniformity, which had not been the case in earlier centuries, in the hierarchy of the church.

All this was something, even if it is not the whole of the story. It was an element or inheritance of unity, to set off against the contrary elements, which events in the ninth century strengthened, of divergence. It meant that, when, later, after the setbacks of the ninth and tenth centuries, Frankish society again resumed its expansion, it carried with it something of a common stock in outlook, in thought and in institutions. England, for example, was affected in the second half of the tenth century, at the time of the reform of the English church by Dunstan, when the introduction of Cluniac monasticism brought English ecclesiastical life more directly into line with that of the continent.[2] The most obvious sign of this influence was the supersession of the native Anglo-Saxon style of writing by the script which we call the 'Carolingian minuscule'. Later also, the influences which penetrated from Lorraine, under Edward the Confessor, and then the Norman Conquest, all implied the extension of Frankish institutions and Frankish ideas and the permeation by them of English society. But the extension of Frankish influence to England was hardly more than incidental: the real thrust was not west, but east and north and south. In the north, it was the church that linked the Scandinavian lands with the west; it was from Germany, from Hamburg, which remained the metropolitan of the north down to the twelfth century, that they were missionized; and the church, because it was a Frankish church, carried with it Frankish ideas and a Frankish outlook.[3] The conversion of Norway and Sweden was completed in the twelfth century by intensive monastic settlement, above all by the Cluniac and Cistercian orders; and the monks of Cluny and Cîteaux carried with them the civilization of the country from which they came.

It was similar in the east, but quicker, because there the missionaries were supported by armies. But in the east the missionaries coming from the Frankish lands were met by similar missions from the eastern church, and this opposition and the failure of the German armies to subdue the Slavs brought the movement to a halt. Thus the Slav lands, to which St Cyril and St Methodius had gone as missionaries from the east between 863 and 888, remained disputed territory – and have remained disputed territory down to this day – between east and west, both politically and in religion and in civilization.

The fact remains that, as the Germans advanced eastwards across the Elbe, they carried with them Frankish institutions, both in church and in state. And it was the same in the south. Here, indeed, Islam more than held its own, down to the beginning of the eleventh century. But when the advance we call the *Reconquista* began, when the reconquered lands, devastated by war, were recolonized by Spaniards and emigrants from southern France, French influence was predominant. Architecture, feudalism, knighthood and chivalry in Spain all bore a French imprint; so that, here again, there was a further expansion of a civilization which had its roots in the Frankish empire.[4]

This expansion of civilization from what we may call a Frankish kernel is the external framework of history for upward of four centuries, from approximately 800 to 1200. Its latest phase, in which it came up against odds greater than it could cope with, was the aggressive wave of colonial expansion which we call the 'Crusades' – an attempt, beginning in 1095, to implant Frankish institutions in their most predatory form in Asia Minor. The crusades were the last echo – before the Spanish conquests in the Americas – of the bloody wars in which Charles the Great massacred the inhabitants of Saxony or forced them to become Christians at the point of the sword. But the failure of the crusades does not detract from the solid results of Frankish 'expansiveness' in Europe. A great deal of Europe is, in fact, impregnated with Frankish institutions and ideas; and the measure of their success lies not in the degree to which they were imposed, but rather in the way in which, later – for example in Bohemia and in Poland – they were voluntarily taken over by rulers who saw the advantages inherent in them. This implanting of Frankish institutions in an ever widening sphere – largely through the subtle propaganda of the church, which carried with it the elements of Carolingian civilization – is the reason why the work of the Franks, particularly of Charles the Great, is of lasting importance. It laid a foundation for the future.

THE CHARACTER OF CAROLINGIAN SOCIETY

It is important, therefore, to have some idea of the nature and character of Carolingian society and of Carolingian civilization.

It was, first of all, a society fundamentally different in outlook and character from that of Merovingian times. Above all, the direct – even if ever weakening – contact with the Roman past, which had been characteristic of all the early Germanic states, had been lost. The only possible exception was those small areas in Italy which had remained under imperial administration until 751, and which at the end of the eighth century were still nominally, if not effectively, under imperial rule. That does not mean, of course, that the idea of Rome had ceased to count. The Roman empire, which had embraced the whole of the world they knew, was for the Germanic peoples – or for the few literate people among them – still a thing of awe and wonder and admiration. But it was, so to speak, a literary idea, formed by reading, or an impression won from the sight of buildings such as the basilicas of Ravenna or the great baths of Caracalla in Rome. It was not a living reality, an integral part of their experience and inheritance. Their society was no longer, as that of the Ostrogoths or Merovingians had been, a crude copy of Roman society as they saw it, drawing on the capital which they had taken over from Rome. That capital had been used up, sucked dry; and Carolingian society had to make do with its own resources.

If Merovingian society was (in Lot's famous phrase) an 'alliance of decrepitude and barbarism',[5] an extraordinary combination of the vices and cruelty and corruption of the under-civilized and the over-civilized, Carolingian society was primitive without the veneer of decrepit civilization; compared with Merovingian society, which was a sort of sterile hybrid, it had fewer pretensions but perhaps fewer of the ills of a pretentious civilization. The nobility no longer aped the Gallo-Roman provincial nobility – which had long since disappeared. Its speech was German, and Charles the Great himself certainly used normally the Frankish tongue. But the upper ranks of society were now, with few exceptions – Charles was one – unlettered, unable to read or to write, and looked down upon reading and writing as the trades of inferiors. Their literature was the literature of song and saga, handed down orally in the vernacular: the exploits of heroes real and imaginary, the legendary Siegfried and the historic Theodoric.

And yet, paradoxical as this may seem, Carolingian society was, in a sense and in a degree that Merovingian society had not been, a clerical society: that is to say, its tone was set by the clergy. This was largely because the literate upper classes of secular society had disappeared. Thus it has often been pointed out that, whereas the typical figure of Merovingian government was the layman, the typical figure in Carolingian government was the great prelate; Charles the Great, for example, when he sent out *missi* or envoys to supervise the local administration in the provinces, relied particularly on bishops and abbots. In the royal court, the work of writing, what we should call the 'chancery' or 'secretariat', was now staffed – naturally enough, since they were the professionally literate class – by the clergy. There is certainly a contrast here, though it must not be exaggerated; there were many aspects of Carolingian society which the clergy and the church were unable to touch. Nevertheless, even in that respect, the church was advancing, seeking for example to reform the institution of marriage and to enforce a more Christian ethic. In this it had, all in all, the support of the state – that is to say, of the king.

For this reason, if we are careful to define what we mean by the term, we can safely say that it was a society in which, by comparison with the sixth and seventh centuries, religion loomed far larger: in fact, one in which gradually, though certainly not before late in the ninth century, a religious imprint was given to society, not in the sense that violence and vice and corruption were less rife – that is not the case – but that even the most violent and licentious paid lip-service to the standards proclaimed by the church, were duly impressed by the perils of hell, were prepared to pay by pious gifts and endowments the price of their sins, and accepted the church's standards of sinfulness. It was a crude religion by any modern standards, but a real one. That it came to dominate social standards was due to St Boniface and the Anglo-Saxon influence, which subtly changed the tone of society.

The change can be seen in the successive rulers themselves. There was, perhaps, never a grosser, more material man than Charles Martel, who was born in the darkest days of Merovingian anarchy; and if he worked with Boniface, it was for political reasons, to extend his control in the German east. But in the case of his two sons, Carloman and Pippin, the position was different. They were imbued in their youth with the new spirit St Boniface brought with him; they were brought up at the famous monastery of St Denis; and both in consequence had a strong sense of the Christian duties of a ruler. And much the same was true, in the next generation, of Charles, though of his youth and upbringing we know nothing, for he was the son of an irregular marriage not blessed by the church. Charles, with his immense vitality, his vast capacity for the pleasures of the senses, his numerous wives and his still more numerous liaisons and love affairs, whose court was famous for its feasts and drinking bouts and its free and easy relations, was the very opposite of a pious or priest-ridden king; but he was, in his own sense of the word, a truly religious one. That is to say, he was determined that, when he came to the last judgment, he would be found standing on the side of the righteous.

Religion, or his own responsibility to God, was a matter of the greatest earnestness for Charles. Few things about him are more astounding than the way this man, who was incessantly engaged in campaigns and fighting, who forewent none of the pleasures of life, spent his time on abstruse questions, deeply engaged, for example, in the intricacies of Easter-tables and the Christian calendar. But for him these were not external matters of detail to be left to others; they were essentials. If you got your Easter-tables wrong, if you celebrated the Passion at the wrong time, might not the whole efficacy of the Easter sacrifice be lost and wasted? What Charles wanted for himself – and insisted upon for his clergy and his subjects – was strict, literal conformity with the letter of the divine law. Theology and speculation were nothing to him; he abhorred them as 'Greek subtleties'. His overriding concern was to find the right course

O rion hab& ftellar in
capite·iii·clafeef·infin-
gulif umerif fingular
clafeef in dextro cubi
to·i·obfcufeem·in dex

and stick to it at all costs, and he had a simple belief that this could be done by well-regulated labour. A happy chance has preserved for us a manuscript in which, at the height of the controversy over images, someone wrote down in the margin Charles's reactions on this intricate subject, and nothing is more astounding than the way in which this man, who knew nothing of theology, set down, like a schoolmaster awarding marks, a 'good' or 'excellent' beside passages from St Ambrose or St Augustine.[6]

In the same way he did not hesitate to reprimand and scold the pope, when he departed from what, in Charles's view, was the correct line. Religion meant for him rigorous conformity, on the part of the pope as of others, with the established usages of the Roman church. He had a fair share of the vulgar superstitions of his age: hence his deep-seated interest in astrology and astronomy – he sent a courier post-haste to Alcuin in the midst of his Saxon wars to find out what it portended when Mars had hurried unduly on its way across the sky and already reached the constellation of Capricorn.[7] But he was determined to eradicate, as a real danger to his own soul and to the welfare of his kingdom, the gross, undisciplined, fervid religion which was all that had survived the Merovingian chaos; a religion typified by the untaught, wandering prophet, naked and dirty, who, to our eyes, appears often to have been regarded as a prophet simply because he was an unbalanced

24 lunatic.

One of the great tasks of government, for Charles, was to discipline religion, to shear it of superstition, to define dogma and ritual which had run off into all sorts of wild aberrations, to reharmonize it with reason and force it to observe established norms. Needless to say, in this he was only partially successful; by the middle of the ninth century, the situation was back where it had been, if not back even further. Like so much else of Carolingian achievement, the reform of church and clergy was only a flash in the pan, and what survived was mere fragments, precedents for the future but not a coherent structure. It was too sudden, too revolutionary, too artificial a change. But it was central to Charles's purpose, and explains much that he did.

For this reason he reformed the liturgy, sending to Rome in 790 for the Roman sacramentary and forbidding the usages of the Gallican church; unity in the forms of divine service meant, for Charles, unity in creed, and it was a proof of true faith when everyone from the north of Gaul to the south of Italy sang the same psalms in the same way.[8] For this reason, again, he set the great Anglo-Saxon scholar, Alcuin, to revise and correct the text of the Vulgate, which had become so hopelessly corrupt through inefficient copying that it was more likely to lead to perdition than to salvation. For this reason he encouraged a reform of writing, in order that through the introduction of a clearer, more legible script – the Carolingian minuscule which, reintroduced in the fifteenth century, is the source of our printed alphabet today – there would be less chance of error in the text of the scriptures, the liturgical books and the holy Fathers. For this reason, above all others, he interested himself in education, hoping in this way to train a generation of clergy learned enough in the scriptures and in theology to avoid heresy and error, and who would therefore be a help and not a stumbling-block in the way of the faithful. Because the teachers were not available in Gaul, he sent for them to Spain and to Italy, but particularly to England, where the school of York provided a model which, through Alcuin, was copied at Tours.

In the same way, something of the learning of the schools and libraries of northern England came to Gaul, either directly in copies of Anglo-Saxon manuscripts or through the commentaries of Alcuin on the books of the Old and New Testaments. Thus the great lights of the ancient church, Jerome, Chrysostomus, Augustine, which had been extinguished in the Merovingian night, began again to shed a beam of illumination. The 'Carolingian Renaissance', as it is often called, the copying of ancient manuscripts, and the revival of letters, was undoubtedly of cardinal importance for the future. It brought together a body of knowledge which, in spite of the setbacks of the later ninth and tenth centuries, was not lost; it set the tone of learning down to the twelfth century, when the transmission to Europe of a new corpus of classical writings by the civilization of Islam opened up new possibilities and a new phase of intellectual advance. Until then – and in many respects long after then – Europe subsisted on the small body of early writers which the Carolingians had made available. How important this is can be seen from the

THAIS   PHAEDRIA   PARMENO

12 The characters illustrated here, under the headings THAIS, PHAEDRIA, PARMENO, are from a ninth century rendering of a comedy by Terence

fact that we can practically count on the fingers of one hand the number of ancient writers – Virgil is the most prominent – whose works exist in pre-Carolingian manuscripts. In other words, our knowledge of Latin literature would be negligible, were it not for the manuscripts copied in the Carolingian era; they were, therefore, the vessel that carried the knowledge and appreciation of Latin Christian civilization to the Middle Ages and to modern times.

Nevertheless, it was essentially a work of salvaging. The Carolingian schools, which Charles ordered to be set up in every episcopal church and monastery, made no significant original contribution. They were concerned essentially with the bare elements of reading and writing, of rudimentary Latin and summary explanation of Biblical texts necessary for the clerical profession. It would be quite wrong to suppose that Charles encouraged scholars like Alcuin of York out of interest in learning or scholarship, still less out of interest in ancient Rome. Alcuin himself had no idea of making an original contribution. Wisdom and knowledge, in his view, were all there at hand in the works of the Christian Fathers. There was nothing his generation could add. All they could do was to tend the field which the Fathers had sowed, make sure that their corn was not submerged and choked by weeds, and garner their fruits. He was, in other words, not so much a scholar, pursuing original knowledge, as a pedagogue, assembling and systematizing. The 'Carolingian Renaissance', as we call it, was simply a by-product of Charles's efforts to raise the standards of clerical education, not as an end in itself, but to reform religion. It was on a par with his efforts to enforce a regular discipline and a collegiate life among the clergy of the great cathedral

27

churches, so that the priests would live a purer life, and therefore better perform their functions.

Charles's belief in the necessity for a sound religious organization, if the state were to prosper, was nevertheless very typical. It expressed a positive attitude to religion which marks the Carolingians off from their Merovingian predecessors, for whom religion, so far as it had counted, had been a flight from the world, the most admirable figure the recluse or hermit. With the Carolingians religion became a force in society; and though this could – and later did – get out of hand, when the power of the state withered and there was nothing to counterbalance a militant ecclesiastical hierarchy, the change was great and the tradition enduring. It persisted, handed down through the east Frankish rulers, to the German emperors of the tenth and eleventh centuries, the Ottos and the Henrys, and finally through them affected the papacy. In this sense, just as it can be said that without Boniface there could have been no Charles, so it can be said that without Charles there could have been no Gregory VII.

The conception of religion, not simply as a means of personal salvation for the individual, but as a social force moving and transforming society, owes its strength to Charles the Great.[9] It is in this sense, not in the sense either that the church was absorbed into the state, or that the state was absorbed into the church, that Carolingian society and – following in Carolingian tradition – medieval society was a religious society. There is no single word to describe the change. To call Charles's government, as is often done, a 'theocracy' creates more misconceptions than clarity. But the fact remains that Charles was crystal clear about his vocation. He it was (as Alcuin repeatedly told him) whom 'the dispensation of our Lord Jesus Christ has made rector of the Christian people'; on him rested 'the whole salvation of the church of Christ'. There was, therefore, for him no distinction of church and state; they were not two distinct bodies, either to be kept severely separate or to be subordinated the one to the other. On the contrary, religion was part of the life of the state, which was founded on divine law; and divine law, which for Charles was identical with the existing canon law of his day, was the state's ultimate rule. This explains the nature of religion for Charles; in his eyes, it was a matter of law and order, and of the due performance of God's commands. And it also explains why from his time religion became the basis of society.

MONARCHY AND ARISTOCRACY

In certain respects, Charles's view of the role of religion implied a return to a more primitive form of society and, in fact, his Christian kingship incorporated not a few of the traits of the heathen king-priesthood of the primitive Germanic peoples. That perhaps is why Charles and his courtiers were so fond of analogies from the Old Testament, why so

frequently his rule was compared with that of the Jewish priest-kings,

13 Carolingian reference to the Old Testament; king David playing the harp, from a ninth-century bible

Melchisedek and David. And in other ways, also, the Carolingian age represents a return to more primitive ways, by comparison with the Merovingian. There is no doubt that, after the dislocation and chaos during the death throes of the Merovingian world, with all the attendant disorganization, agriculture again went forward; the eighth century was a time when more land was brought under the plough. But on the other hand, society was now essentially an agrarian society; severance from the commercial life of the Mediterranean seaboard brought fundamental changes in the economy. And the political changes were much the same in character. The thin Roman superstructure had gone. The remnants of Roman bureaucracy had given place to a more primitive government in which the king's personal following, his household, looked after his interests as best it could. Otherwise, society was held together, not by any common allegiance to the state, but simply by the bonds of man to man, the duty owed by a man to his lord, the obedience enforced by the wealthy landed classes, who claimed and exercised inherent rights to govern. Land was now the source of wealth and political power, and the governing society was an aristocratic society of wealthy equals.

Inevitably this also affected the king's position. Fundamentally, in spite of unction and the belief in the mysterious virtues of royal blood, the king was only the wealthiest and greatest of the nobles. His position depended on his landed wealth, and only so long as he had wider estates and a greater armed following than any of the aristocracy would he be able   29 to maintain his position at the head of society. Naturally, the king struggled against this, if he had anything about him at all, in order to build up his position, and to turn the aristocracy of wealth into an aristocracy of service, which owed its prerogatives and position in society to its loyalty to the crown. He also tried to offset the power of the aristocracy by fostering and protecting other classes of the population – notably the common freemen, the free peasantry – who would look to the king as their master and protector and not to their immediate aristocratic lords, as did the servile tenants. Some kings also sought to use the church as a balance or equipoise against the nobility; but this was not so often the case, nor was it so easy as is often supposed, because ever since the sixth century the higher ranks of the church had been permeated by members of noble families. Bishops and abbots were members of the aristocracy and it was difficult, if not absolutely impossible, for anyone who was not a born nobleman to rise to episcopal rank; and the interests of church and aristocracy were more often identical than opposed. Hence one may fairly say that, in general and in the last resort, when all else failed, the king was thrown back on his own resources.

Therefore the history of the kingship at this period, and for centuries to come, is really the history of the king's estates, of the royal demesne, or (as it was still called, in Roman parlance) of the 'fisc'.[10] When the demesnes were large and productive, all was well with the monarchy; when they were divided up among different sons or branches of the royal family, when they were given away to favourites or (by pious kings) to the church, when the local administrators were not kept under control, and allowed to turn the lands and revenues to their own profit, when in short the 'fisc' was 'dissipated' or 'dilapidated', then there was trouble. If nothing were done to remedy it, by resumption of crown lands or by further conquests, then it might lead to the displacing of the existing dynasty by a new royal line. In any case, the crux was land, land-tenure, the wealth that went with land, the tenants and followers and retainers which accrued to a man with wide estates.

Furthermore, this society, depending on land-tenure, was a proto-feudal society. It was not, perhaps, a feudal society by comparison with the ninth and tenth centuries, but it was a feudal society by comparison with the sixth and seventh centuries, by comparison with Merovingian times. The change had begun in the time of Charles Martel, and under his son, Pippin III, and his grandson, Charles, the process of 'feudalization' continued without interruption. It continued in spite of the fact that Charles, seeing the possible dangers, tried in some respects to put on the brake. Not, indeed, that Charles was opposed to feudalism as such, for there was no question of an 'anti-feudal' policy. The antithesis 'feudal – anti-feudal' is a modern antithesis. On the contrary, the Carolingian dynasty had come into the saddle through the strength of the feudal

14, 15, 16 Carolingian society: kingship, the church, the peasant

bonds which made them, with their following of vassals, far more powerful than the shadowy Merovingian kings. One might almost say that they won the throne as the representatives of the 'feudal principle' and of a feudal organization of society; and Charles the Great never turned his back on this legacy.

So far as Charles could use feudal bonds to build up his own power, by increasing the number of his own vassals and using them both in his army and to administer his conquests for him, he showed no hesitation. Indeed, he could not do otherwise: it was the only way of getting the work done. The concentration of wealth in land, the sharp decline of fluid wealth with the collapse of commerce, the limited quantity of money in circulation, precluded – even if he had thought of it – the reconstruction of a non-feudal hierarchy of salaried officials. In this sense, and for this purely practical reason, feudalism was the very backbone of Carolingian government; there was nothing to take its place. But where, and when, feudal developments seemed inimical to the interests of the monarchy, naturally enough an attempt was made to check them. To take but one example, the Carolingians had risen to power at the head of their *antrustiones*, their armed following. What more natural than that they should seek to prevent the rise in the same way of competitors, who might challenge their own position? Therefore, in 779, Charles issued a capitulary forbidding the formation of a *trustis*. This edict has often been taken, along with others, as evidence that Charles had an 'anti-feudal' policy. The truth is much simpler. Charles's standard was purely practical. He encouraged what would strengthen his position, whether it was what we today should call 'feudal' or not; and in the same way he discouraged what was, or seemed to be, against his interests, no matter whether 'feudal' or not.

These purely practical considerations explain what seem at first glance to be inconsistencies in Charles's policy. They explain why, on the one hand, we find him to all appearances organizing an official hierarchy which, in our eyes, seems to have the sole purpose of holding the feudal aristocracy in check, and on the other hand stimulating the growth of feudal bonds, which seems to us to weaken the official hierarchy. In fact, under Charles, feudal and non-feudal measures supplemented each other. The obvious candidates for the 'official' position of count, or for the envoys (*missi*) sent out to travel the country supervising the counts, were the royal vassals in whom the king had personal trust, and who were closely tied to him by the personal bond of vassalage and by the fact of land-tenure. It was not a question, as it seems to us, of two contrary and mutually exclusive methods of ruling – either through a feudal hierarchy or through non-feudal officials – but simply the practical task of enlisting every means at hand to get the job done. In the late Merovingian anarchy, public authority had suffered an eclipse; and the business of Charles the Great, and of his father and grandfather before him, was simply to reconstitute that authority, not to impose a particular preconceived type of government. All we can safely say is that this obvious, practical end would be governed by the means; in other words, that the sheer impossibility of paying a large bureaucracy, or factors such as the difficulty of communications, would tend to force the king, whether he liked it or not, to rely on his vassals in practice.

Carolingian legislation, on the other hand, tended to dwell on the other, non-feudal aspect – naturally enough, for feudal relations were governed and regulated by a series of separate agreements between individuals, rather than by general rules, and were only exceptionally reduced to writing. Therefore Carolingian legislation tends to be deceptive; it gives us a distinctly one-sided view, from which many modern accounts of Carolingian society and Carolingian government suffer. Nor, of course, was legislation always effective. It tells us more of intentions than of what really occurred, and there is little doubt that the reality of Carolingian government was very different from the picture which the edicts or capitularies present. Above all, the feudal element, the reliance on feudal means, loomed far larger. The anarchy of late Merovingian times had let loose a 'drift towards feudalism', the subjection of the weaker to the stronger, a search for protection and a surrender of liberty in exchange for protection. What the Carolingians did was to organize and stabilize and consolidate this incoherent feudalism, at any rate sufficiently for it to cease to be a danger to order, and if possible so that it would become an effective instrument at the disposal of the ruler.

In some ways, to stabilize and consolidate meant to check; and there is no doubt, for example, that Charles tried to safeguard the position and multiply the numbers of the smaller freemen, who still owed no duties to a lord. He saw in them, without much doubt, a counterpoise to the power of the nobility. On the other hand, there was, in the circumstances of the day, no more obvious or effective way of exercising control over the individual – and therefore of checking tendencies to lawlessness and self-help – than through his lord. Consequently at every stage of the hierarchy the lord was made responsible for his men; he had, for example, to produce them, if required, at the county courts before the king's representative, the count; and finally, in a capitulary of 810, a general order was issued to the effect that every *senior* (that is, everyone of importance) was to compel his *juniores* (that is, those dependent upon him) to better obedience of the king's mandates and precepts.

This is a good example of the way in which Charles used feudal bonds, which had grown up spontaneously, outside the law, in response to social and economic conditions, as a means to more efficient government. The feudalization of society was a fact no ruler could afford to ignore. Though it might be possible, as we have seen, to favour the dwindling class of freemen as a counterpoise against the aristocracy, the free class, except for the wealthy nobles, went on dwindling. For one thing, the expense of bearing arms was more than the free peasant could support, particularly as heavily armed cavalry became the order of the day. Charles tried to meet this situation by allowing the free peasants   33 to join together in groups, each of which had to send one fully armed warrior to the army. But such an expedient could not hide the fact that the ordinary free peasantry was declining in numbers and in economic importance, that fighting was becoming a closed profession, and that ultimately – in France at least – only those who fought would be regarded as free and noble.

That, however, was not the case in Carolingian times; it only occurred during the tenth century. For that reason Carolingian society was not exclusively a feudal society, and the king still had other means of government than feudal ones at his command. But the growth of feudalism was so strong that those other means were very limited in effect; and we may certainly say that, by the beginning of the ninth century, feudalism was the backbone of Frankish government. Down to the death of Charlemagne in 814, however, it was a feudalism pretty thoroughly controlled by the king. It was not 'anarchic feudalism' (as it is sometimes called), in which each feudatory fought and struggled and existed simply for himself with no control from above; it was not a society in which authority had been fractured by feudal tendencies, in which there was only so much authority – or brute force – as each feudatory exercised in his own area, but no cohesion or co-ordination. That stage came later. As long as Charles the Great was on the scene what is remarkable was the subordination of feudalism to the king's purposes and the way it takes its place, with other non-feudal elements, in the scheme of government. Thus, for example, the old public courts of hundred and county still remained in existence; they had not yet been transformed into or superseded by feudal courts, though there is no doubt that, outside the public courts, which were courts for free men, and for free men only, the feudatories exercised jurisdiction over their dependants. What is significant is not that the two things existed side by side, but rather the way that each reinforced the other. That is what was so characteristic of the government of Charles the Great: it was not a perfect instrument; there were many abuses, a great deal of raw force and even violence; control was intermittent and extremely difficult to maintain, and one senses all the time, and particularly in the last half of the reign, the effort required to keep it functioning. Nevertheless it worked because every means of government was subordinated to the purposes of the monarchy, and because they were so woven together that each strengthened the other and all were actively employed by the state.

FROM KINGDOM TO EMPIRE: THE CAROLINGIAN EXPANSION

If we ask ourselves why this was so, the answer will lie not in any significant degree in Charles's personal qualities as a ruler, but above all else in the great impetus, the expansive energies which carried the Frankish forces forward in a victorious onrush for some eighty years, beginning with the series of campaigns in 716, 717 and 719 by which Charles Martel established his power and position in the Frankish kingdom. This advance may be compared, not unfairly, with the other great onrush of

34

the Salian Franks, almost similar in duration, between the accession of Clovis in 481 and the death of Clothar I in 561. It was on a bigger scale, but it had something of the same rather hectic, unstable character. As Clovis laid the foundations by destroying the other Frankish sub-kings in Gaul, so Charles Martel laid the foundations by his campaigns against the opposition at home, and the hardest victories were the early ones, which had to be won again and again; then, the consolidation completed, the onrush against the enemy outside began, and the superior organization due to the development of feudal armies made it easy for the Franks to prevail over less advanced peoples.

Frankish expansion, the expansion of the rule of the Frankish kings, was really the use of a superior organization to subject other more primitive folk, whose governments were less efficiently organized for war. The victories were usually easy; the difficulty was to enforce the victory, to devise a permanent means of control. This was done only by a gradual wearing-down process, in which, as the Frankish church was reformed and reorganized, it played a leading part, but which had to wait for that reorganization which really got under way only after 741 and took twenty years or more to become effective. Aquitaine in the south-west, for example, was subdued in 720; but the work had to be done again by Pippin III. The position was substantially the same in the east, in Swabia and Thuringia and Bavaria, where the independent Bavarian duchy was not finally suppressed until 788, and replaced by more direct government by Frankish counts.

This, in general, was the line of attack: to displace the local or native ruling class by a Frankish aristocracy, whose interests were bound up with the interests of the monarchy. It was a typical policy of a conquering people, and we find that exactly the same process occurred in England, for example, after 1066. The aristocracy owed its position, the new lands and revenues which it acquired in the outlying provinces, to the conquests carried through by the king; and so they were bound together by a community of interests. This community of interests, this concentration of energies on conquest and then on exploiting conquest, underlay and explains the Frankish success. Whereas, under the Merovingians, crown and aristocracy had been at loggerheads and had paralysed each other – thus producing anarchy – conquest and expansion gave their successors a common motive, which overcame dissension. A similar situation can be seen in England under Edward III. There again, king and barons united against France, and the conflicts which had caused civil war under Edward II were forgotten; but when Edward III's campaign against France failed, internal difficulties and unrest began again.

It was the same under the Carolingians. Nothing succeeds like success. So long as conquest and expansion were possible – and conquest and expansion meant, of course, tangible profits, new wealth, the possibility for the king of endowing new vassals, the absorption of the estates of conquered rulers, such as the Lombard kings of Italy – there was nothing to worry about; and without any doubt the impression we have of the Carolingian state, of a great machinery of government working efficiently without creaking and breaking down, is due first and foremost to this fact. Unfortunately this has been too little realized. Historians have written of Carolingian government as though it were something fine and efficient in itself, whereas in reality what kept it going was not any virtue of its own, but simply the military conquest and expansion which accompanied it until just after the year 800.

Carolingian government, as we shall see, was not very efficient. It worked just as long as expansion continued, that is, just as long as it could call on new resources; but once it had to work within stabilized boundaries, and even more once it was faced with contraction, it started to creak, and all the difficulties, which had not been solved but had simply been brilliantly overridden, came out into the full light of day. This is usually attributed to the incompetence, the personal weaknesses of Charles's successors after 814. We are given the picture of an efficient machinery of government wasted and ruined by inefficient rulers, with the implication that if only Charles could have gone on living for ever, or if only a second Charles had succeeded him, all would have been well. Actually, the trouble started a good deal earlier, certainly within a year or two of 800; and Charles's later years were beset by clouds and shadows.[11] It is important to realize this, because otherwise our picture of Carolingian government will be out of focus – it did not go on, almost perfect, until 814, and then break down owing to the deficiencies of Charles's son, Louis the Pious. The weaknesses were already inherent in the structure, which (as I have said) was an amalgam of divergent forces held together only by external successes. Once the unifying force of common effort in a great wave of aggression was removed, and its place taken by defence of contracting frontiers, the fragility of the structure of Carolingian government became apparent.

It is easy to exaggerate the military success of Charles the Great. Within the lands which had of old belonged to the Frankish kingdom he had no great difficulties; after the defeat and deposition of duke Tassilo of Bavaria in 788, these countries accepted the Frankish yoke, but there the main work had been done for him, the backbone of resistance broken, by his father and his grandfather, and the church did the rest to bind them to the Frankish kingdom. His victory in Lombardy in 774, which made him king of the Lombards as well as king of the Franks, was also overwhelming, an immensely impressive *Blitzkrieg* won in a matter of weeks. But Pippin's earlier Italian campaigns had shown how little resistance the Lombards were able to offer; and the explanation of the Frankish success lies for the greater part in the internal disunity of the Lombard kingdom, where, from the beginning, the monarchy was weak and feudalism had made no headway. Against the concentration of forces made possible by feudalism in Frankish Gaul, the disunited Lombards were helpless.

When we look beyond this, however, the position is very different.

For example, Charles's expedition against Muslim Spain in 778, bringing him up against an efficient military power, was a shocking failure; and thereafter Charles kept at a respectful distance, building up the Spanish march of Barcelona as a rampart between him and the Moors. Moreover, the conquest of Lombardy was not an unmitigated advantage, for it brought him in the south into contact with the forces of the Roman empire, and again he could make no headway. Indeed, here he was immediately involved in new complications; for the Byzantine government continued to recognize the Lombard princes who had taken refuge in Constantinople, and to support the Lombard duke of Benevento in the south of the Italian peninsula, who retained his independence. It was, in fact, to subdue Benevento – another campaign that was a failure – that Charles went to Italy on the expedition in 800, when the pope made him emperor. Here, therefore, both on the Spanish and on the south Italian frontiers, were two 'running sores', in which Frankish strength was wasted with no result. And yet no vital Frankish interests were involved in the south, and wise statesmanship would have suggested concentration of efforts north of the Alps.

The vital interests of the Frankish monarchy lay on the eastern frontier, in Germany, not in Italy; and the south was only a distraction. There is some evidence that Charles himself realized this. His reign had opened with a *rapprochement* between the Frankish and Lombard monarchies. When in 773 the difficulties between the Lombards and the papacy, which had caused Pippin to intervene earlier, again broke out, Charles's first thought was to avoid hostilities; he even went so far as to offer the Lombard ruler a substantial payment of fourteen thousand gold pieces, if he would settle with the pope peaceably. Only the Lombard refusal of this offer brought Charles into Italy in 774. But even after his conquest of Lombardy in 774, his visits to Italy were infrequent: the first, made unwillingly and only at the pope's urgent request, in 780, the second in 785, the third and last in 800; and it is characteristic that, after his return to the north in the spring of 801, he never again set foot on Italian soil.

The reason is obvious: Italy was a 'by-activity', an unwelcome diversion. In 772 Charles had begun his effort to subdue the Saxons; and the Saxon wars lasted, off and on, from 772 to 804, a full generation, absorbing all his energies and efforts before they were brought to a successful conclusion. There is little doubt that, in these circumstances, Charles would have preferred to leave Italy alone. Furthermore, the Saxon wars were accompanied simultaneously by the wars with the Avars, whose power reached from Hungary to the borders of Bavaria; and Charles's campaign against Bavaria in 788, when the Avars had leagued with the Bavarian duke against the Franks, showed him that, if his control of Bavaria were to be secure, he must deal with the Avars also. Thus from 791 to 796 he had this further complication on his hands; and though the destruction of the power of the Avars cost less effort than the subjugation of Saxony, the two undertakings together imposed a heavy strain on Frankish resources.

17, 18, 19 Charles the Great's empire was secured through the momentum of military success. Left, a military figure of the early ninth century; right above, a war scene from a contemporary manuscript; right below, Charles investing Roland with the Spanish March (from a twelfth-century manuscript)

Interrogatio sacerdotis.

Forsahhistu unholdun . Ih fursahhu.
Forsahhistu unholdun uuerc.
Indi uuillon . Ih fursahhu .
Forsahhistu allem then bluostru
indi diderigelton. Indi diderigotum thie
im heidene man zigeldom . entazigo
tum habent. Ih fursahhu .

Gilaubistu ingotfater almahtigan Ih
gilaubistu inchrist . Igilaubu .
gotes sun nerienton . Ihgilaubu .
Gilaubistu inheilagangeist Ihgilaub .
Gilaubistu einangot . almahtigan .
Inthrinisse . Indiineinnisse . Ihgilaub .
Gilaubistu heilagagotes chirichun Ihgil .
Gilaubistu thuruhtaufunga
sunteono forlaznessi . Ihgilaub .
Gilaubistu lib aftertode . Ihgilaub .
Exopeizatur malignus spiritus ut
exeat etpecedat danrlocumdo .

Exi abeo sps inmunde etredde
honorem do uiuo etuero .

Accipe signum cruciscristi tam In
fronte quam Incorde. Sume
fidem caelestium preceptorum .
Talis esto moribus; ut templum di

20 Copy of the baptismal vow imposed on the Saxons after their defeat in 804

21 Sea-power enabled the Vikings to mount their raids against the Frankish empire; right, head of the wooden stem-post of a Viking ship

The Saxon wars, it is clear in retrospect, were the real turning-point of Charles's reign. He was successful, though only through brutal, ferocious treatment; but when in 804 Saxony was at last pacified at the point of the sword, the population forced to become Christian or massacred or transported, the Frankish effort was spent. The year 804 is not merely a turning-point in Charles's reign; it is a watershed in Carolingian history. The limits had been reached; expansion was at an end; thereafter there were no more successes; and from that moment nothing went well. The coronation of Charles as emperor in 800 involved him in a 'cold war', naturally enough, with the legitimate Roman emperors in Constantinople. From 803 to 812 this 'cold war' turned into a real war in Italy between Frankish and Byzantine forces, but in spite of victories Charles had no real hope of final success, and in the end a compromise peace was patched up.

Simultaneously two new enemies came on the scene: in the Mediterranean the Saracen privateers who attacked Corsica and Sardinia and ravaged the coast of Italy; in the north, both on land and sea, the Vikings. Against both, in the last resort, the Frankish empire was helpless, because it had no navy and no idea of the importance of sea power, and so the enemy could always escape to return again. But the Danes were also a menace on land, for the Frankish kingdom had a common frontier in the north with Denmark, and Danish attacks across the frontier were frequent. Moreover, the conquest of Saxony had brought the Franks up

41

against the Slavs, beyond the Elbe, and soon Slavs and Danes were in league against them. The Danish king claimed that he would soon be in Charles's capital Aachen, with his army; it was freely rumoured that in a short time he would control the whole German east.[12] And the Franks, in sum, could do nothing except take up the wearisome task of defence against a foe whose next unexpected place of attack they could not foresee. To push on further into the wild Slavic east was impossible; at the river Elbe they had reached the natural limit of expansion, and yet were no more secure.

Inevitably, as they went over uneasily from attack to defence, as the conquerors found themselves the attacked, the tone among the Franks changed and trouble began at home. Charles's later capitularies, from 807 onwards, have a sorry tale to tell: famine, wandering beggars, bands of outlaws and robbers, speculation, usury, high prices, disobedience, refusal to serve in the army, resistance to Charles's officers, complaints of oppression by officials and exploitation of the poor by the rich. People were tired of war, thirsted for peace and social reform;[13] Charles himself, no longer the successful leader of an incomparable army, lost his popularity.[14] And at the court itself, whose poets had so confidently sung Charles's praises, there was a significant change of temper. The poems of Theodulf of Orléans are the writings of a bitter critic of his contemporaries, who awaits God's judgment on their sinfulness, and is convinced only that he stands at the end of time. 'The walls which in our youth stood fast, artistically painted, are full of cracks, the sign of coming dissolution. Just as it irks an old man to sing and make merry, so all sweetness has left the ageing world and nothing remains of its former strength.' Thus Theodulf; it is an epitaph on Charles and his reign.

THE IMPERIAL CORONATION

Down to 800 and beyond, to the climax in 804, the spirit had been different. There is an immense, almost vulgar, self-confidence and self-esteem about the Franks in their period of expansion, comparable only to that of the armies of the French Revolution or of the Germans after 1871. They felt that they were God's chosen people, that the extension of the boundaries of their kingdom was proof that God favoured them. This feeling was expressed by the poets. The court poet, Dungal, praising Charles's prowess against duke Tassilo of Bavaria, traced back his descent to the Trojans. The Saxon poet says that the Romans took years to conquer Italy, but Charles did it in a trice, and also conquered other peoples of whose names even the Romans were ignorant. Another proclaims that, even if you had all the cohorts of Rome to help you, even if you had Odysseus and Achilles to help you, you would be a fool to fight the Franks; for the Franks are a people second to none in valour.[15]

This is crude stuff, with all the emphasis on superiority in war; but it is typical. It is the boastfulness of a young, expansive people. They were as good as the Romans; indeed, they were better; for Rome had fallen, and now Charles, the Frankish king, ruled where Rome had ruled. In fact,

Warnfried goes further, pointing out that Charles had conquered Rome that was once head of the world.[16] Thus the Franks were not continuators of the Roman empire; they superseded it. And if they outstripped in this way the legendary emperors of antiquity, how much more did they outstrip the other rulers of their day. Nowhere is this sense that the Franks have risen into the first rank better expressed than in Alcuin's famous letter of 799, in which he compares Charles and the pope and the emperor to the manifest disadvantage of the latter two. The pope had just suffered mutilation at the hands of his enemies, and been driven out of Rome; the emperor had been deposed by his own people; but Charles's royal power was untouched – the 'royal dignity' in which Jesus Christ had set him up as rector of the Christian people. Charles was thus more excellent in power than the other two dignitaries of the Christian world, more distinguished in wisdom, more sublime in his royal dignity; indeed in him alone, Alcuin concludes, rests the whole salvation of the church of God.[17]

This famous comparison expresses better than anything else the sense alive among the nobles and clerics at the Frankish court of the exalted position which their successes down to 799 had given them. They were second to none; they claimed equality of status with the two greatest powers of their day, the emperor at Constantinople and the caliph Harun al-Rashid. Charles's relations with Harun have, no doubt, a practical explanation: he wanted co-operation against the Muslims of Spain, who had rejected the caliph's authority, and he wanted co-operation against the old enemy of the Arabs, the emperor. But we can safely say that the diplomatic exchanges with Baghdad show more than this: they show the Franks claiming and taking a place among the leading powers of the Mediterranean world.

Their attitude towards Byzantium was similar. There has been much controversy about Charles's assumption of the title of emperor. Direct evidence that he ever planned to usurp the role is entirely lacking; but he did claim equality for his kingdom with the Roman empire, and was not prepared to accept a second place. This is seen above all else in the sphere of religion. The old tradition, going back through Justinian to Constantine, that it was for emperor and pope between them to settle matters of doctrine for the universal church, was totally unacceptable to him. Why should they? The pope was continually imploring his help; the emperor, since 751, was totally unable to help the papacy; Charles himself, by his conquests against the heathen Saxons and the Avars, had done more than either to extend the bounds of Christianity; and in any case, what title had the emperor in Constantinople to direct the doctrine of the church in the west, which was totally outside his power and control? As the head of the Frankish church, Charles looked on such claims as an injury, and the issue came to a head in 787 when the pope and the imperial government came together to settle the long-standing dispute about images and the council of Nicaea, the seventh ecumenical council, was called together.

The council of 787 signified an adoption by the imperial government, which had taken the lead in iconoclasm and thereby lost favour in Italy and the west, of the western point of view; it agreed, in a carefully thought out formula, to permit not indeed the worship but at any rate the honouring of images. The pope was naturally delighted, and gave his authorization to the decrees of the synod. Not so Charles. Not that the particular doctrinal issue had any outstanding significance for him, or that he and his theologians really understood what the issue was. For him the significant point was that the pope and the emperor had dared to ignore him.[18] His theologians were quickly put to work to provide a counterblast, and the result was the 'Libri Carolini' which appeared between 790 and 792. In them the council of Nicaea was condemned as not representing the universal church; its decrees were denounced as 'things arrogantly done in Greece'. More particularly, however, the actions of the emperor – who, significantly, was refused his title and addressed simply as king – were challenged. His pretensions to regulate the doctrine of the universal church, he was told, were heretical; it was simply a continuation of the attitude of the ancient emperors, whose empire was the most unrighteous the world had ever seen.

But this tirade was not enough. The work of Nicaea must be undone; and so in 794 Charles summoned a synod at Frankfurt, which was to be the genuine ecumenical counterpart to the false synod of Nicaea. Here the pope, who does not come out of the story too well, was forced to eat his words and betray his convictions through the legates whom he dared not refuse to send. The council itself was presided over by Charles in person; standing before his throne, he set forth the position, bullied the participants, had the first and last word. And he carried the day. The adoration of images was condemned; the pope's representative dared not raise a finger in support of the doctrines he had wholeheartedly approved seven years before; and, above all, the might of the Frankish king, and the equality of the Frankish kingdom with the empire, was made clear before the whole world. Indeed, more than this, Charles had shown that he was the Christian ruler above all others, and as such higher, at all events in the eyes of God and of the righteous, than the emperor. The emperors, Alcuin said, ruled by the precepts of the Romans; but 'for us' – that is, for the Franks – the precepts of the Bible were more important.

This extraordinary sense of divine mission, which had become the very marrow of the Frankish kingship since the time of St Boniface, the sense that to Charles rather than to pope or to emperor God had entrusted the government of Christendom, the overweening pride in Frankish achievement and success, all contributed to make possible the conferment on Charles of the imperial title by the pope in 800. They were the preconditions without which the idea could scarcely have arisen. But they were not the cause. After the Caroline Books and the synod of Frankfurt, it looks as though the imperial title was a natural culmination; but that was not the case. First of all, the very attitude of the Frankish court to the empire, which we have seen, should serve as a warning.

22 An idealized portrait of Charles the Great; from Einhard's *Life* of Charles
23 Irene, ruler of the Byzantine empire from 797 to 802

The contempt for the empire, the gibes at the Greeks, the sense that Charles's kingship, as a Christian kingship, was far and away above any empire in this world – and this as late as 799 – were not easily compatible with any desire on Charles's part for the imperial title.

In fact, Charles's biographer, Einhard, who had the best means of knowing, says flatly that if Charles had known what the pope intended to do, he would never have entered the church of St Peter in Rome on Christmas day 800, when the act of coronation was carried out. Historians have tried to twist Einhard's meaning, but it is safest to take his words at face value. If one thing is certain, it is that the initiative for the imperial coronation did not come from Charles's side, and that it was not for him or in his eyes or those of his contemporaries the culmination of his achievement. In fact it played no part in his plans and, neither before nor after 800, in the shaping of his policy. Its origins must be sought in another direction, in another chain of events; or rather in two chains of events, closely connected, the one in Constantinople, the other in Rome itself.

In Constantinople, as we have seen from Alcuin's remarks, the situation was disturbed and gloomy. Power was in the hands of a woman, Irene, who had blinded and deposed her son, Constantine VI, and had actually, for the first time in the whole of Roman history, taken the title of emperor, 'basileus', for herself. But her position was insecure – she actually fell from power in 802 – and there were conspiracies and revolts and civil war. In Rome, the position was much the same. Here the starting-point was the death in 795 of pope Hadrian I. The longer he had lived, the more Hadrian had been disquieted both by Charles's dictation of ecclesiastical doctrine and policy and by his reversion, in Italian territorial affairs, to the policies of the Lombard kings, and he had, therefore, so far as possible, **45** drawn nearer to the imperial government in Constantinople. Consequently, on his death, the Franks had put in as successor a minor and faintly disreputable figure, who took the title of pope Leo III. But Leo also, as a Frankish nominee, came in for a good deal of hostility among the Roman aristocracy, and there is not much doubt that this opposition party, which actually broke into rebellion and seized and deposed Leo in 799, was in touch with Constantinople.

Thereafter events came thick and fast. First, Leo escaped and made his way to his protector Charles, who was directing military operations at Paderborn. Then Charles, who was preparing to go to Italy himself for a campaign against Benevento, sent Leo back with a commission to inquire into the charges against him. The decision of the commission, so far as we can see, was probably political. Leo was accused of perjury and adultery, and the charges were probably true – at all events Alcuin burnt the documents in the case for fear lest anyone should see them. But since it was considered unsuitable that the holy pontiff should be subjected to earthly judgment, he was allowed to clear himself by oath, and on 23 December he was reinstated. Then two days later, on Christmas day 800, Charles went to St Peter's for the service at which his son was to be consecrated king by the pope, and there, while Charles was kneeling in prayer, the pope placed on his head a golden crown, and the Roman people who thronged the church acclaimed him as 'Charles, the august, crowned by God, great and pacific emperor of the Romans'. The pope then knelt down and went through the gestures of adoration traditionally offered to an emperor.

In this way, Charles became emperor. The forms were the regular forms. The acclamation of the people was the regular constitutive act, representing election by the Roman people. The crowning and adoration by the pope were less essential, but it was usual at Constantinople for the patriarch to do the same. And there was nothing in the law and constitution of the empire which laid down that the elevation of the emperor should take place at Constantinople. It could take place in Rome, which was still part of the empire in 800, or anywhere else.

These briefly are the facts. Far more complicated, and more disputed, is the interpretation; but the main features are reasonably clear. First, there is no doubt that the real actor in the drama was the pope. It was in his interest that the coronation was carried out. It was, of course, made possible by the powerful position of the Frankish king; that is to say, unless the Franks had by now had a predominant position in the west, and a power in Italy which no one, least of all the emperor in Constantinople, could challenge, it would have been unthinkable. But we must not confuse the preconditions of an event and its causes. The same applies to the situation at Constantinople. The extraordinary position there that a woman had taken the imperial title for herself, and the circumstances in which she had done so, made it possible to hold that Irene was a usurper, and that the imperial throne was vacant. But here again we have only a pretext, not a cause – Charles was not elected because Irene

24 St Peter with pope Leo III on his right and Charles the Great on his left;
after a ninth-century mosaic

was a usurper; the reasons lay in events in Italy and essentially in Rome.
They lay in the pope's need for protection.

But this too involves a chain of events leading back to the driving-out
of the imperial exarch of Ravenna by the Lombards in 751. Until then,
the natural appointed protector of the pope had been the exarch. After
754 the Frankish ruler had stepped into the gap and, as a religious duty,
given the pope his protection. But the Frankish presence was weak and
undefined, and the revolt at Rome in 799 had shown that this somewhat
indefinite protection, which did not rest upon any clearly defined legal
basis, was not enough. Therefore, if we approach the question by asking
ourselves *cui bono*, the person who most obviously gained was the pope.
'For him', it has been said, 'it was an assurance of more powerful protection, and better authorized', if his protector, who had simply had the
nebulous, ill-defined title of 'patricius', had the title of emperor and the
right to exercise the emperor's sovereign powers at Rome. In those
considerations,[19] very limited in their scope, we have, I think, the real
explanation of the coronation of 800.

For Charles, on the other hand, the advantages were far less clear. Historians of all shades of opinion agree that the imperial title brought no change in his policy and no change in the organization of government. As we have seen, he never went to Italy again after 801. He retained his independent royal titles: that is to say, he still remained king of the Franks and king of the Lombards. His kingdoms were not absorbed into, nor became part of his 'empire'. There was, in short, no change of orientation after 800. The most that can be said is that 'his consciousness of his responsibilities towards God and of the religious character of his authority is accentuated'.[20]

But it is not easy to find evidence in support of even this attenuated hypothesis. With the Caroline Books and the synod of Frankfurt of 794 in mind, it is difficult to think in what respects the religious aspects of Charles's authority needed strengthening or could be strengthened. On the credit side, therefore, there is nothing to suggest that he had any reason to seek the imperial title. After as before 800, the solid foundation of his power remained north of the Alps, where he continued to rule as king. On the debit side, on the other hand, there is a great deal to indicate what he lost by the coronation. Above all, he was involved for the rest of his reign (or, at any rate, until 812) in a niggling dispute and a series of wars with Byzantium which wasted his resources and diverted his attention from the serious Danish threat in the north, and which were a constant worry and distraction of his old age. For naturally enough the imperial government in Constantinople was not prepared to recognize the legitimacy of Charles's position. For Constantinople he was a usurper, neither more nor less, an anti-emperor set up by a faction in one of the remotest provinces of the empire. So the Byzantines stirred up war on his southern frontier in Benevento and sailed a fleet into the Adriatic which weighed anchor in the laguna of Venice, and commenced hostilities there also.

Far from being sought after by Charles, the imperial coronation was rather in the nature of a coup d'état engineered by the pope. Moreover, it was a short-term manœuvre, an 'improvisation' engineered as a result of the rebellion of 799.[21] Because of that the pope saw the need for substituting, in place of the hostile imperial government which was still the ultimate authority in Rome, a friendly power. Hence, profiting by the confusion caused by Irene's deposition of her son, he set up Charles as 'anti-emperor', in the knowledge that the imperial government, which had not effectively intervened in Italy for half a century, would be able to do very little about it.

In itself, therefore, the event had very little historical importance: rather, it was a desperate expedient in a difficult situation. It is doubtful whether, even on the pope's part, it was intended to have lasting, long-term results; it was simply a manœuvre to keep his head above water, and it was sufficient for his purposes if it succeeded in this aim. There is also no doubt that Charles himself regarded his new title simply as a personal dignity which was 'destined to disappear with his person' on

25 Charles the Great depicted with his son Pippin, who died in 810

his death.[22] That is shown most clearly of all in the testamentary disposition he made in 806, dividing his lands on his death among his three sons; there was no question of passing on the imperial title to the eldest son, still less of the maintenance of the 'unity' of his 'empire'. Personally Charles in 800 – so he seems to have thought – had acquired a new dignity, perhaps because God looked on his work with favour; but it was, and remained, a personal dignity; he was emperor as well as king; but the title did not extend to his successors, and it did not extend (and that was even more important) to his lands. Charles himself became emperor; but the lands over which he ruled did not become an 'empire'. The kingdom of the Franks, the kingdom of Lombardy remained in existence, as they had been before.

There is, therefore, no question of the creation in 800, as has so often been said, of a 'western empire', or of a 'revival' of the Roman empire in the west. The pope, as a subject of the emperor, rose up against the existing emperor, whom he regarded (or pretended to regard) as illegitimate, an anti-emperor. This had nothing to do with the west; it all took place within the boundaries of the existing empire. And there was no question of the creation of anything new. In the lists of emperors which have come down to us, Charles is not the first ruler of a new empire, but the sixty-eighth emperor after Augustus, following on after Irene, to whom, therefore, he was regarded as successor. Thus the coronation of 800 was a domestic event in the history of the Roman (i.e. what we call the Byzantine or east Roman) empire, and in that context not a very important event; for often enough before, and often enough afterwards, the government had to cope with anti-emperors, raised up as the nominees of rebellious factions. But the point is nevertheless important. It means not only that a new 'western' empire was not created in 800, but also that the later 'papal' theory of the empire of the Middle Ages, according to which the pope gave the 'empire' to Charles, or transferred the empire from the Greeks to the Franks, and could therefore take it away again if he saw fit, does not correspond to historical reality.

49

And yet, effectively, by the time Charles died in 814 a 'western' empire *was* in existence. How, if it was not 'created' in 800, did this come about? The answer is that it was the result of events between 800 and 814. The coup d'état of 800 had, as we have seen, immediately placed Charles in a difficult position in relation to the legitimate imperial government in Constantinople. We may accept the statement of the earliest Frankish authority after the event[23] that Charles, with his deep religious sense, regarded the pope's action as the will of God, to which he could only humbly – if sometimes rather irritably – submit; he was not prepared to give up the title simply because of Byzantine opposition. On the other hand it was highly desirable, if only to try to avoid unwanted military complications, to seek some sort of agreement or arrangement with Constantinople. Consequently negotiations began immediately; and in the end they were successful, because also in Constantinople, at this very time hard pressed by the Bulgarians on the Danubian frontier, the whole business was an undesirable complication which the Byzantines would have liked to bury decently, if they could do so without loss of face.

There is no need to follow the course of negotiations in detail. They started, it would seem, with a proposal for a marriage and some sort of 'condominium', or joint rule over the imperial lands, by Charles and Irene; but this proposal was killed by the deposition of Irene in 802. Her successor, Nicephorus, dug in his toes, was far less conciliatory, and the result was a suspension of negotiation and the wars in Venetia and Istria and Dalmatia which have already been mentioned. Then in 812, and this time definitely because of Bulgarian pressure, negotiations began again. It was a sign of the great store Charles set on getting a settlement with Byzantium that, having on the whole been successful in the fighting and having conquered Venice, he agreed to give up all his conquests to date, and also to renounce further conquests in Italy (that is, south Italy, including Sicily and Sardinia, which consequently henceforth remained Greek). In exchange the Greeks, skilled diplomats adept at driving a hard bargain, made one concession and one concession alone: they recognized Charles's title of emperor. But even this was done in deliberately vague and empty terms. Charles was 'emperor', but it was not stated what he was emperor of. In other words, his title remained a personal dignity; and above all he was not *Roman* emperor. For just as there was only one Roman empire, so there could only be one Roman emperor; and that was obviously the legitimate emperor in the east. The claim to rule in the Roman empire conferred on him by the pope in 800 was given up by Charles, and was not again claimed by any ruler in the west until the close of the tenth century.[24]

That the Roman empire of the west dates from 800, or even from 812, is, therefore, not true. But in the negotiations of 812 with Constantinople a new phrase was introduced, if only unofficially. This was the 'imperium occidentale', or 'western empire', which was contrasted and put on an equality with the eastern empire.[25] Even this was an equivocal phrase, of dubious meaning. Moreover, it was not an official title and neither

Charles nor any of his successors ever, in their diplomatic correspondence, used the phrase as a formal description of their lands. Nevertheless the settlement of 812 is important. It meant, first of all, the end of the chapter opened in 800. That was all over and done with; a line was ruled across the ledger; the claim that Charles was emperor 'governing the Roman empire' was a thing of the past. It meant, secondly, the beginning of an empire which was not 'Roman', but which was vaguely described as 'western'. This, without doubt, was something; it was at least a satisfaction for the Frankish claim, going back (as we have seen) many years before 800, to equality with the Roman empire. Whereas, previously, right down to 812 there had been one empire, and only one, after 812 it was publicly agreed that there were two, and one was in the hands of the Frankish king. Thirdly, the source of this new dignity was important. In 800, the emperor had – whatever the theory – received his dignity at the hands of the pope. In 812, when he dropped the title illegitimately conferred on him in 800, he got his new imperial title by his own exertions and sacrifices, by the territorial concessions which he made to Constantinople for recognition. Therefore he owed his 'empire' – whatever significance we may attribute to the term – to himself, and to himself alone. Unlike the abortive title of 800, which was 'Roman' in character and Roman in origin, the title of 812 was 'Rome-free'. And finally, unlike the title of 800, which was only a usurper's claim, no more effective than that of 'bonny prince Charlie' to be king of England in 1745, the title of 812 was internationally recognized.

For Charles himself 812 evidently had special significance. Hitherto, as we have seen, he had treated his title as a personal honour which would die with him, and there are no directions either in his testament of 806 nor in that of 811 for disposing of it after his death. But the agreement of 812 changed all that, for it now gave him a title which was his, not conferred on him by the pope and the Roman people, and with this he could do as he wanted, for he now had an independent position. Therefore in 813 he reversed his previous attitude, and had his surviving son – the others had died in the meantime – raised to imperial rank, so as to secure the succession. Furthermore, the method by which Louis was raised to the rank of emperor is also significant for the light it throws on Charles's attitude. In 800 Charles had been acclaimed by the Roman people, and crowned by the pope. In 813 nothing of the sort occurred. The elevation of Louis took place not in Rome, but in Aachen, the chief seat of the Frankish monarchy; and it was essentially a secular act. It was, moreover, essentially a Frankish, not a Roman, act and the pope was not even represented. Charles asked the Frankish nobility, who had been summoned to the great council, if they agreed to his handing over to his son the imperial dignity; and after they had agreed, it was Charles himself who placed the crown upon his son's head.[26] It was the custom of the Byzantine court that was being followed; and it is quite evident that the contrast with 800 was not accidental. Clerical participation was deliberately excluded. Charles was emphasizing the autonomy

of the imperial title he had secured in negotiation with Constantinople, and carefully distinguishing it from the illegitimate title of 800. By carrying out the act at Aachen with the participation of the Frankish nobles, he showed clearly that it was the 'western' or 'Frankish' empire that was handed on to Louis, not the 'Roman' empire of 800.

What the content of the new dignity was to be was still an undecided question. Charles in the last two years of his life, weary and ill, never got so far as that, and probably had no desire to embark on anything so controversial. The achievement of securing a recognized title, placing the Franks on a level of equality with Rome, was enough; and it was left to Louis, his son, to show whether the empire was to mean anything politically – whether it was to give rise to an imperial policy, which it certainly had not done under Charles – or whether it would remain, as it was at Charles's death in 814, a personal dignity, proud and exalted, but not affecting the structure or government of the Frankish lands.

So far as the history of Charles's reign is concerned, we can almost say that the empire and the imperial title made no difference, except in so far as it involved him in disagreeable complications with Byzantium. For a few months between 801 and 803 he really seems to have thought that God had marked him out to be ruler of the Roman empire; there is the faint breath of a new spirit in his capitularies of 802.[27] Then, with the rupture of negotiations with Constantinople in 803,[28] we are back where we were. Thereafter, there is no sign of new ideas; 'as emperor Charles simply continues the work commenced before 800'.[29]

The coronation of 800 was, therefore, neither the culmination nor the crux of Charles the Great's reign, as has so often been alleged. The crux, as we have seen, had been the termination of the Saxon wars in 803. When the imperial question was finally settled in 812, it was too late to make any difference. Ever since 804 there had been ominous creakings. The contrast between the reign of Charles and that of his son, which used to be drawn, as though there was a sudden collapse in 814, is not true; much that was to be characteristic of Louis the Pious's reign had its beginnings in the last decade of Charles's.[30] The great successes turned to failures, without any period of solid, stable achievement in between. But the decline which set in after 803 was at the same time a gathering of forces for the future. The unified structure of the Carolingian state, with counts and bishops spread far and wide and serving the king who was the keystone, was predicated upon success and conquest and expansion. Once conquest ceased, other factors came to the fore without delay, and shaped the course of events. Therewith we pass out of the reign of Charles, which joins the eighth and ninth centuries, and partakes of both, and come into the ninth century.

26 Interior of the Palatine Chapel, Aachen, begun *c.* 790

Three   **The decline and fall of the Carolingian empire**

THE NINTH CENTURY is apt to get short shrift from historians. Compared with the reign of Charles the Great, through which there seems to run one main thread, namely the concentration of Frankish power, the ninth century gives the impression of breaking up into meaningless confusion, of which it is difficult at first glance to make anything positive. There is no obvious thread, as there had been until 804, holding the history of the period together; in the welter of civil wars, dynastic conflicts and intrigues, few things stand out as significant. It is therefore treated all too often as a sort of interlude, a period of setback and decline, when the achievement of Charles the Great was ruined; and historians jump as quickly as they can from the 'great' age of Charlemagne to the 'great' age of Otto I.

This view is nevertheless short-sighted. Approached from the point of view of political history, of kings and dynasties, the ninth century is, indeed, a pointless confusion of mediocre names. The significant changes go on, so to say, under the surface. But, if we probe beneath the surface, we soon find that the ninth century is of fundamental importance in European history. The historian who, writing on the ninth century, gave his work the title 'The collapse of an empire and the birth of a Europe', put the matter in a nutshell.[1] The empire put together by Charles the Great was a failure; it had no future; it simply petered out, leaving no direct inheritance. The shape of European history hereafter was not to be that of the Carolingian world. Precisely because Charles extended the boundaries of Carolingian power so wide, to the Elbe and into Austria, into the mountains of Carinthia and down to the gulf of Venice, never again would it be possible to contain the whole in one political organization. Frankish conquest fractured the mould of Frankish government; it was like the serpent that died of swallowing more than it could digest. Consequently the Frankish empire – by which I mean simply the total agglomeration of lands under Frankish rule – belongs irretrievably to the past, perhaps the last of the long series of ancient empires beginning with Egypt and Assyria and continuing with Alexander and Rome; and it was from the post-Carolingian world, in the course of the ninth century, that Europe arises.

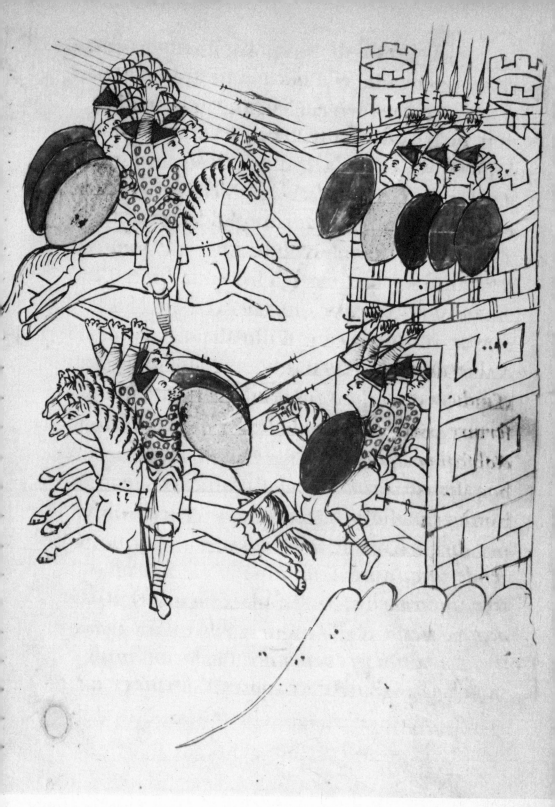

27 Warriors attacking a fortified town; from a tenth-century manuscript

In this sense the ninth century is far nearer to us than the age of Charlemagne, which thought of itself as the culmination of the ancient world, and had the haunting fear (or hope) that the end of time was just round the corner. A thread runs out from the ninth century to the present in a way that it does not from the eighth century. That does not mean, of course, that the age of Charlemagne left no inheritance at all, that it died without any after-effect. Above all, it created a myth, which grew and was incorporated in the famous legend of Charlemagne – a legend which even today tends to overshadow the real man.[2] In the second half of the ninth century, when decline was apparent on all hands, men looked back to the 'empire' of Charles as a time of peace and prosperity and unity, a 'golden age' which they only needed to recover for all to be well. It was a legend which badly corresponded to the facts; but in history legend is often more potent than reality, and it created the idea (or perhaps, the ideal) of the unification of Europe, of all the people of Europe, in one Christian community of peace, under one government. This idea, or ideal, remained to counteract the opposite tendency to diversity, which sprang from the hard fact of the diversity and different origins of the various European peoples; and although earlier the same idea of unity had been bound up with reminiscence of the 'universal' government of Rome, after the ninth century it reflected above all else the 'unity' created by Charlemagne.

In detail, also, as we have already seen, much else was handed down from the Carolingian world – for example, a framework of administrative organization so that it can truthfully be said that government in feudal Europe had its origins in Carolingian government. But it is also true that much of the Carolingian achievement was short-lived and ephemeral, and all that survived were fragments and precedents for the future, but not a coherent whole. Or, as another historian has put it, 'there is no complete succession to the institutional hereditaments of the Carolingians. Some things descend, some are changed, and some pass into desuetude. In no province or country will we find the story quite the same. In no place is the process simply the substitution of count or bishop for king.'[4]

What survives, in short, is bits and pieces which are taken and put into another context, used for new and different purposes, Carolingian in origin but no longer serving the purposes of Carolingian government. But the Carolingian achievement, the concentration of forces around the crown, which is what makes Charles the Great's reign stand out, was ephemeral. The Frankish empire did not remain 'a going concern';[5] and when we come to the beginning of the tenth century, a hundred years after the death of Charles, the picture is totally different, the structure permanently and irretrievably changed. The separate states of Europe are crystallizing out, the map of Europe is beginning to take on a discernibly 'modern' aspect, the very weakening of superior control has released and given free play to new forces, which had been held in check; and as a consequence society is transformed from top to bottom. That is what takes place in the ninth century, and continues in many parts of

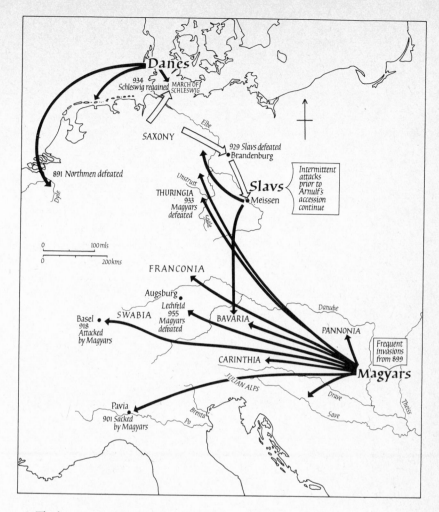

Danes

934
Schleswig regained MARCH OF
SCHLESWIG

Elbe

SAXONY

929 Slavs defeated
Brandenburg

891 Northmen defeated

Dyle

Unstrutt

Slavs

THURINGIA
933
Magyars
defeated

Meissen

Saale

Intermittent
attacks
prior to
Arnulf's
accession
continue

0   100 mls

0   200 kms

FRANCONIA

Augsburg

Lechfeld
955
Magyars
defeated

Danube

SWABIA

Basel
918
Attacked
by Magyars

BAVARIA

PANNONIA

Frequent
invasions
from 899

CARINTHIA

Magyars

JULIAN ALPS

Drave

Pavia
901 Sacked
by Magyars

Brenta

Po

Save

Theiss

28 The late stages of the 'barbarian invasion' of the Frankish empire

Europe into the tenth; it is where the fundamental importance of the period lies. When we see that, and see what to look for in the ninth century, then its history becomes intelligible and significant.

INTERNAL TENSIONS AND EXTERNAL THREATS

If we ask why the achievement of Charles the Great was ephemeral, we come immediately to a series of factors which were to be of major importance in shaping the future:

1 The achievement of the Carolingians up to 804, as I have tried to show, was predicated upon success. When success eluded them, there was no solid foundation strong enough to withstand adversity and misfortune.

2 Charles had acquired an imperial title, but there was no imperial government; the title had not resulted in any transformation of Carolingian institutions, and the problem of ruling an empire – i.e. lands outside the immediate Carolingian homeland – was never fairly and squarely met.

3 The 'empire' after 814 raised new problems and created new internal tensions; it did not add new strength to Carolingian government. Potentially (as it seems to us) a new element of 'unity', it worked instead in the direction of disunity, and that just at the moment when greater unity was necessary in the face of gathering difficulties.

4 The machinery of Carolingian government was too rudimentary for the immense task of governing the new conquests. Lombardy was conquered, Bavaria subjugated, the Avars crushed, Saxony mopped up; but then the real problem began – namely, to establish an efficient and lasting administration. Each subjugated area had its own past, its own history, its own institutions. It was in some sort of way a unity. Consequently each conquest introduced new tensions – this time tension between the existing society and the Frankish or Carolingian administration superimposed upon it.

5 To these internal strains, new pressure from outside added external strains. Charlemagne, in the last decade of his reign, had been faced by Danish attacks in the north and Saracen attacks in the south. These attacks gathered weight in a crescendo in the course of the ninth century, and to them were added later in the century and in the early years of the tenth century, the attacks of the Hungarians or Magyars from the east. This is often described as the last wave of barbarian invasion, and it was in fact the last serious pressure of the sort on western Europe until the appearance of the Mongols in the middle of the thirteenth century, although eastern Europe – particularly the Roman empire in the east – had to meet the threat of the Seljuk Turks in the eleventh century. The simultaneous invasions of Saracens, Vikings and Magyars were, so far as the Carolingian realm was concerned, the last straw. If they had fallen on a strong united state, it might have been able to withstand them. But they fell on a state already weakened by internal tensions, and the result was to aggravate all the tendencies to disruption which were already there.

These, briefly, were the main factors at play in the century after the death of Charlemagne. Their consequence, when they had had their effect, was a complete transformation of the Carolingian world.

THE WEAKNESSES OF CAROLINGIAN GOVERNMENT

The key to the whole situation lies in the character of Carolingian government; because, if it had been as efficient, as well organized and as highly developed as it is often said to have been, the breakdown and the subsequent course of developments would be very difficult to understand and to explain. It is, unfortunately, far too easy to reconstruct from the legal sources a picture of Charles the Great's government, which makes it look like a great uniform bureaucratic administration; and it is only in recent years that historians have begun to see how deceptive and misleading this picture is. It is deceptive because, as I have already emphasized, there simply was not the fluid wealth in existence to maintain a bureaucracy such as existed contemporaneously in Byzantium and in the caliphate of Harun al-Rashid.

It is misleading, also, because such a picture obscures the real forces behind Carolingian government. It is true that the count was the pivot of Frankish government, and the first step in taking control of a conquered area was to substitute Frankish counts for the native ruling classes. But it is not true to suppose that the count was an 'official', and still less true to suppose that the Frankish lands and Frankish conquests were divided out into uniform administrative districts, called 'counties', which the count administered. The count was not an 'official'; that is to say, he was not paid a salary – which for us is the mark of an official – but was assigned lands for his upkeep and also took a share (usually a third) of the profits of the area under his control, which gave him an obvious interest in exploiting the people over whom he was set. Nor (and this is no less important) did he have an administrative staff of 'officials' working under him. The evidence shows us that (in the west, at any rate) he usually had a deputy; that there was a clerk to keep the records of the county meetings; and that, over and above that, there were three to six hundredmen, responsible to the count, and in charge under him of the hundreds, which were grouped together to make up a 'county'.

The county, therefore, had no real 'corporate' existence; it was simply a periodic meeting, which only existed in the form of the county court, and characteristically the Latin word for 'county' and for 'county court', the word *comitatus*, is the same. What we call 'local government', therefore, really took place in the hundreds, and these to all intents, were autonomous, self-governing. Of course, orders were transmitted to them through the count to produce men or to provide money, to pursue thieves, and so on; but the actual execution of these and other tasks was their affair, and this really of necessity, because there was no 'bureaucracy' to do it, and in case of refusal or insubordination, the only recourse was to collect a military force and conduct a military expedition to enforce obedience.

In the whole Frankish kingdom after the conquest and inclusion of Saxony there were in all some 250 counties – and so 250 counts at most, for some counts certainly functioned in more than one county – and if each had a maximum of ten assistants, the sum total is a 'staff' of 'local officials' (as we should say) of around 2,500 – and that for an area comprising the whole of modern France and western Germany and Italy from Rome northwards. But, of course, they were not local officials. A good deal is known of the personnel of the counts, who represented Charles in this way in the provinces.[6] They were nearly all noblemen who were his vassals – royal vassals, or the vassals of the royal demesne, the *vassi dominici* – many of whom were in fact connected by blood or 59 marriage with the Carolingian dynasty; and the bulk of them came from the Austrasian lands along the Moselle and the Meuse, from which the dynasty itself hailed. Thus there was in effect a thin Frankish stratum of conquerors superimposed on the conquered countries; people of rank, great noblemen, whom the king knew personally and trusted; but a very small and select group. To speak of them as 'officials' is wrong; they were feudatories, but feudatories close to the king, vassals of the royal dynasty.

That is why, as I have said before, it is an error to distinguish, in Charles's government, between the 'official' and the 'feudal' hierarchy: it was the same men in both cases, counts who were vassals, vassals filling the position of count. But what kept the government going, what made it effective, was their loyal service. Without them the 'county organization' would have remained a skeleton; they gave it life. Charles did not rely for government on a 'system', or a division of duties among a bureaucracy of officials, but in essence upon the services of his vassals. So far as we can see, he could and did remove them and change them at will; they had no inherent right, based on the tenure of land, to their positions; they did not necessarily succeed from father to son; and in that sense the government was different from later feudalism. The king's hands were not tied. But basically, if he wanted to get things done, he was thrown back on his feudal dependents, the demesne vassals; and in this sense one cannot escape the conclusion that Carolingian government, to this degree, was already feudal.

That such men, chosen in this way for their personal qualities, had a good deal of discretion, that the king, because he knew and trusted them, left them in the main to run things as they thought best – not so much supervising them and subjecting them to control, as simply removing them if they failed or betrayed his trust in them – needs no emphasis. Here again, in fact, he had not much choice, for material conditions – not merely lack of monetary resources, but also the fact that there was no fixed capital of the kingdom – made the development of an organized central government impossible.

In regard to 'central institutions' (in itself a misleading term), there has been as much exaggeration as in regard to 'local government'. There was, for example, no 'civil service', no clerical staff, no secretariat, no 'chancery', such as we find in European states after (but not before) the end of the twelfth century. Such writing as was done – and we must assume that most orders were transmitted verbally – was an incidental job of the clerics who performed the religious services in the king's chapel. The maximum number in any one year (and they were not all necessarily at work at the same time) was five clerks and one superintendent, – a fantastically small number for the written work of an area so huge.

The still more important branch of finance was even less well organized and more under-staffed. There was nothing comparable with the specialized services and the differentiated ministries, each with its hier-archy of officials, which existed contemporaneously in Constantinople or Baghdad. The idea of a 'central government' functioning without the king, of a routine of administration with bureaucratic control, was totally lacking. It was, like the 'local government', all far more personal, very different (for example) from the centralization of the *ancien régime* in France in the seventeenth or eighteenth centuries, with which sometimes, quite erroneously, it is compared. For there an organization existed whose function it was to direct, instruct, control the *intendant*; in Carolingian government there was no such permanent central bureaucracy.

The 'central government' – if we choose to use the term – was simply the king's household; that and nothing else. It looked after the king's resources, the king's interests, but it did not govern the 'state' – indeed, the Roman conception of the 'state', as something distinct from the king's personal patrimony, his 'privy purse', had for all practical purposes disappeared. Ministers, to whom whole categories of business could be deputed, did not exist. Consequently the king himself had to make all decisions; and his sheer physical inability to cope with more than a tithe of the questions arising was itself a major limitation. To say that Charles's 'will penetrated to every corner of the kingdom' is perhaps true enough in the exceptional cases where he actually intervened; but such cases were highly exceptional. It was only when complaints became loud, when local extortion and repression provoked a violent reaction, that he knew what was going on, and might then act.

For the most part, however, what is characteristic of Carolingian government is not central control but the lack of central control. Here, even the famous institution of the *missi dominici*, royal envoys sent out to supervise the local governors and to suppress abuses, which owed its regularization to Charles's own initiative, made little difference. Potentially, no doubt, it was a step forward; that is to say, it created the possibility of some sort of permanent control which might have been developed and extended. But in fact it never was developed into a permanent institution, an institutional link between the king's court at the centre and the local government. The fact that it was in 802, and only at that late date, that the sending out of special commissioners was 'regularized'[7] is significant. It was, in short, one of the first of the emergency measures to meet the growing disorders of Charles's later years.[8] And what it was in origin, it remained: a stop-gap measure[9] introduced because of the growing evidence that the counts were getting out of hand.

The *missi* did not become a normal, regular element of Carolingian government; and that means that there was no special link, no machinery to secure cohesion between the centre and the provinces. So far as control was asserted, it was not through institutional means, but through personal influence and pressure. The great men of the kingdom, counts and bishops to the fore, had to attend the assemblies of magnates in May and in the autumn, the solemn courts or 'great councils'; and it was here that they were instructed, rebuked, and, if necessary, dismissed.   61

This annual or twice-yearly meeting with the king – to remain absent from which without good excuse was tantamount to rebellion – was the only really effective means of control. For the rest, the king relied first and foremost on the bonds of vassalage, on the fact that the counts were 'his' men, who owed their wealth and importance largely to his favour, and whose lands, held of him, were the final pledge for their good behaviour and loyal attitude.

He also relied, and for long with good reason, on their rational self-interest; namely, on the fact that, as strangers representing the Frankish interest in distant provinces, they had every reason to remain loyal to the Frankish, which was the royal, cause. And as long as Frankish expansion and conquest were going on, he could count on their desire to share in the conquests. But time necessarily weakened these ties. Conquest ceased: Families which had been simply foreign agents – in Lombardy, for example – settled down and gradually identified themselves with local interests, which might well not be the interests of the king. When this occurred, the Carolingians had nothing to put in the place of the bonds which were wearing thin; nothing because they had deliberately relied on personal bonds as the sinew of government, because they did little if anything to cultivate the loyalty of the conquered peoples, preferring to rule them through Frankish agents; nothing, above all else, because, despite appearances to the contrary, they did not build an administrative system capable of running under its own steam.

In this respect, the achievement of the Carolingians was extra-ordinarily barren; no one, down to and including Charles the Great, seems to have had any idea that the vast extension of Frankish territory required new means of government and above all a far more complex administrative apparatus. Frankish government in 800 was hardly different in character from that in the time of Clovis;[10] and Charles never seems to have felt the need for anything more complicated. For him it was simply a personal question, a question of personnel: if he recruited good counts, good government would be assured. Beyond that his imagination did not reach. So far as he was compelled to adapt himself to the new conditions, it was not by remodelling the scheme of government, but by throwing a heavier burden on his vassals and trust-ing to the bonds of vassalage to hold together.

THE IMPERIAL QUESTION

It was a very inadequate foundation for the future; and there is evidence that some of the more discerning men of the time were aware of this. A few months after Charles's death, the archbishop of Lyons, Agobard, laid before his successor, Louis the Pious, a plan for legal reform, pro-posing to replace the different legal systems in use among the different peoples of the Frankish dominions by one legal code for the whole empire.[11] This revolutionary scheme was not put into effect; but Louis, in his early capitularies, did something to reduce the legal diversities which reflected the fundamental disunity of the empire.[12] Far more important than this, from the beginning of his reign Louis adopted a positive attitude to the empire and to his own imperial title, quite different from that of his father. The very fact that this occurred immediately on his succession is significant, indicating a deliberate breach with the past, and suggesting that Louis had around him a group of advisers dissatisfied with Charles's attitude and determined to give the new imperial title, acquired in 812, a concrete meaning.

The change of attitude was immediately registered in Louis's title; and though this may seem a mere formality, it was, in reality, symbolic or programmatic.[13] Charles, as we have seen, had carefully retained his royal titles, king of the Franks and king of the Lombards, thus proclaiming the autonomy of his two kingdoms and the fact that they were separate from the 'empire'. Louis, from the beginning, suppressed his royal titles and used only the title of emperor. This change reflected the programme of a ruler, aware of the defects of the existing organization of government, who was determined to do two things: first, to make the empire a reality, which it had never been under Charles the Great, and secondly to use the idea of one empire as a means of establishing unity throughout the Frankish lands. Thus from 814 the imperial question becomes a major question of politics, in a way that it had never been under Charles, the reason being that for Charles the 'empire' had remained throughout a personal dignity, something distinct from the Frankish state, which had not affected Frankish government; whereas under Louis it came to represent a principle of Frankish government.

Louis's conception of what the empire was dated from 812 and from his own elevation to the imperial dignity in 813, in which, as we saw, neither the pope nor the Roman people had any hand. For Louis the empire was evidently not a 'Roman' but a 'Frankish' empire; that is to say, it was the complement of, or counterpart to, the 'Roman' empire in Constantinople, the equivalence and parallel position of which had been recognized in 812. It represented in his mind the sum total of lands under Frankish rule, and was the common bond between them, offsetting their differences of origin and history. Not by chance did Louis put on his seal the legend *Renovatio regni Francorum*, an inscription that accurately reflected his plan and programme: to renew or give new life to the Frankish kingdom through the idea of empire. It is significant that contemporaries now began to use the phrases 'Frankish empire' and 'emperor of the Franks', although this title was never official. But it described accurately enough the current conception of what the empire was and what it stood for.

Louis's conception of the empire was made particularly clear when, in 817, he set down his dispositions for the future government, his testament in the event of his death. This ordinance of 817 is the counterpart of Charles the Great's ordinance of 806, and the differences are characteristic. In 806, Charles partitioned his dominions among his three sons, in accordance with traditional ideas of the division of the royal patrimony; there was no mention of the 'empire' or the 'imperial title', and 63 no idea, apparently, of maintaining the unity of the Frankish conquests. In 817 Louis also made provision for his three sons, but the destructive idea of partitioning the inheritance was avoided. The two younger sons, Pippin and Louis, were to have kingdoms, the one a kingdom of Aquitaine, the other a kingdom of Bavaria, while Charles's grandson, Bernard, to whom he had given the kingdom of Italy in 813, was maintained in his position. But these kingships were subordinate powers of government under the eldest son, Lothar, who was proclaimed emperor with rights over the whole of the Frankish dominions and who was to be the sole inheritor of his father's imperial position. The younger brothers, for example, were precluded from pursuing their own independent foreign policies; they were neither to conclude treaties separately nor to send and receive embassies. The subordinate kingdoms represented, therefore, little more than a measure of 'administrative devolution' within a single empire; the unity of the whole was maintained, and the different parts were to give each other military support, if necessary, against foreign attack. In this way the empire provided the link between the whole vast agglomeration of lands; furthermore, as a result of the superior position of the emperor in relation to the kings, the ideas of primogeniture and indivisibility were introduced. From the point of view of the future, the advance between 806 and 817 was startling; it was really a new idea of the state which came into existence.

But Louis's conception of the empire as a link or binding force between the different parts of the Frankish lands provoked attack from two sides. Perhaps it was too rigid in application, and applied with too little flexibility. It was, it has been said, only practicable 'on condition of being realized by stages'; and it is possible that it was because Louis and his advisers were determined to impose their plan without delay, that they ran into trouble.[14] In any event, opposition quickly came to a head, first from the pope, and second from the Frankish aristocracy.

The opposition of the pope was cautious and slow-moving. There was no head-on challenge, because the papacy had little effective material power to oppose to the strength of the Frankish emperor, but it was effective in the long run, once internal difficulties, arising from the opposition of the aristocracy, had neutralized the royal power and, by creating opposed parties in the Frankish lands, had given the pope the chance of making allies. The internal opposition found a handle in dynastic quarrels, in the dissatisfaction of the sons, and then of the grandsons, who were – or saw themselves as – cut out of their rightful inheritance; and many accounts push the sordid dynastic and family quarrels into the foreground, as though the personal issues were the real rock on which the Frankish empire split.

In fact, the dynastic issues were little more than a peg, or a pretext, on which the real issues were hung. The real issue was between the new conception of a unitary empire, as set forward programmatically in 817, and the traditional Frankish notions of a patrimonial state. The opposition which arose was a conservative opposition, defending traditional

29 Lothar, son of Louis the Pious, was made emperor of the Frankish lands in 817, but civil war followed and by the treaty of Verdun in 843 Lothar was awarded only one-third of the kingdom

ideas against royal innovation, and it is significant that the leaders of the opposition, when the crisis came to a head, were the advisers of Charles's later years, who had been dismissed in 814. That indicates best of all where the crux lay: it was a struggle of the old régime, which had no use for the new-fangled ideas of 'empire' – a Frankish party, which saw salvation not in change, not in reform, and not in religious revival, but in the maintenance of Frankish hegemony over the conquered lands and over the church and papacy, in the spirit of Charles.[15]

Papal opposition arose from the fact that the empire, first by the settlement of 812, then by Louis's coronation of 813, and again by his second coronation in 814, had been cut off from Rome. A Frankish empire, with its seat in Aachen, not in Rome, was no use to the papacy; indeed, its independence might make it positively dangerous. Against this danger, the papacy cautiously but progressively reacted, seeking to re-establish the links with Rome that had snapped in 812, and playing upon Louis's genuine religious convictions to bring him back under papal authority. These efforts were helped by a growing tendency, already evident in Alcuin's writings, to regard the empire as a 'Christian empire', *imperium Christianum*, an attitude from which Louis himself was by no means free. They were helped, secondly, by the growth – already in Charles's later years – of a reform party, inspired by St Benedict of Aniane, which saw in the unity of the empire a guarantee of 'the liberty of the churches, the security of their possessions and the equitable distribution of their resources'. This party was the strongest force from the beginning of Louis's reign to the death of Benedict in 821, and almost inevitably favoured the re-establishment of a close connection with the papacy; and the death in 816 of the disreputable Leo III, whom Charles to the end had treated with the utmost disdain, created an opportunity.

Leo's successor, pope Stephen IV, took the initiative, crossed the Alps – like Stephen II before him in 754 – and persuaded Louis to receive benediction at his hands and to be crowned still once more, this time by the pope himself with a special crown brought by the pope from Rome. Thus the link between the papacy and the empire was re-established, in the spirit of 800. But the coronation of 816 was only a first step, tentative not decisive. In the very next year, 817, Louis had his eldest son, Lothar, made emperor in exactly the same way as he had been made emperor by Charles in 813: that is to say, at Aachen, by the acclamation of the assembled nobility, placing the crown himself upon his son's head. Nothing final, therefore, was achieved by Stephen IV. But he set a precedent; and the precedent was soon confirmed by events. Lothar himself, crowned emperor in 817, allowed himself to be persuaded by the pope to be crowned again in Rome in 823; and this was still a further step, connecting the empire not only with the papacy, but with Rome itself, and so making Rome the seat of the empire. The empire was brought back again, first within the orbit of the papacy, then within the orbit of Rome.

66   Within a few months the course of events made this result definite.

When in 829 revolts broke out in the Frankish lands, and Louis the Pious's sons rose against their father, the papacy's chance came. In 833, pope Gregory IV entered the contest on the side of Lothar against his father. He was welcomed by some as the saviour of the empire, condemned by others as a fomenter of rebellion; in reality he was staking out a claim to a decisive voice between the different pretenders, and opposing his authority, the *sacra iussio apostolicae sedis*, to the *sacra iussio imperialis*.[16] Soon a strong party, reacting against the civil wars in the imperial camp, came to look to the pope as the only arbiter who could restore peace and unity to the empire. At the same time the different competitors angled for papal support, and sought coronation at the pope's hands as an argument for claiming that their authority was superior to that of their rivals.

In this respect the reign of Lothar's son, Louis II, was a turning-point. Louis II was twice anointed (844, 850) and three times crowned (844, 850, 872) at the hands of the pope, and these repeated acts seem to have established the precedent that the pope alone had the right to carry out the consecration of the emperor.[17] The practice of the father elevating his son to the imperial dignity died out, and after 850 there is no further instance of the creation of an emperor save at Rome and by the pope.[18]

This gradual consolidation of the pope's position prepared the way for the pontificate of pope Nicholas I (858–67), indisputably the leading personality of his age in the west. The period of Nicholas I saw the rapid development of the papal theory of the empire, which was now accepted even among influential circles in the Frankish lands which had earlier resisted this view and had clung to the Frankish conception of the empire – or the conception of a Frankish empire – which had its roots in the events of 812 and 813. Even in the time of Nicholas I, this older theory had important adherents, notably archbishop Hincmar of Rheims; but it was undermined by the civil wars, and from the middle of the ninth century the clerical view of the empire as an instrument of the church, and particularly of the papacy, for the government of Christendom, began to prevail.

In so far as a Frankish idea of the empire, independent of the papacy, continued to exist, it lost the significance and content which Louis the Pious and his advisers had tried to give it, and became merely a claim to hegemony of one Carolingian pretender over the others, and particularly a claim to control the disputed territories between east and west, that is, the Rhinelands with Aachen, the territories to the south linking the Rhineland with Italy, and Italy itself. It no longer represented a cause or a programme. That change was the result of the ninth century; and it was a momentous legacy. The restoration of the connection between the empire and the papacy set the stage for some of the major conflicts of the next centuries: the conflict of pope Gregory VII and the emperor Henry IV; of pope Innocent III and the German claimants, Philip of Swabia and Otto of Brunswick; of Innocent IV and Frederick II. Naturally these later conflicts had a different historical context, but their roots lay in the ninth century, which left Europe with two conflicting theories of empire, and no solution to the imperial question opened in 800. In this respect, as in others, the ninth century was formative.

CIVIL WAR AND PARTITION

What made this astounding papal success possible – astounding when we consider the abasement of the papacy in 799 – was the outbreak of civil war in the Frankish lands in 829. The starting-point was an event which seems, and in itself was, trivial: the second marriage of Louis the Pious, the birth in 823 of a fourth son, Charles, and the demand – in itself reasonable enough – that the arrangements made in 817 for the succession should be modified in favour of the new son. That so obvious a demand should have led to civil war is only explicable in the light of the existing party divisions.[19] These divisions had existed in embryo from the beginning of the reign, when Louis got rid of his father's advisers, whose loyalty he did not trust; and basically it was the division between a 'reform' party, which wanted the institution of an effective imperial government, and a conservative party, composed mainly of the high aristocracy and the bishops, who had been the real beneficiaries of Charles's government, holding all the main offices, and who wanted nothing changed.[20]

The crisis came to a head in 829 when Louis, in the face of all opposition, decided to make a new division, creating for his son Charles an apanage in Alsace. This was inevitably at the expense of the eldest son, Lothar, for his two brothers, Pippin and Louis, had been provided for in the east and west; and Lothar allowed himself to be drawn into rebellion, followed immediately by his two brothers who feared that if they did not also act their claims and rights would suffer. Louis capitulated, and promised to be governed henceforward by the advice of the magnates – a clear indication of the real motives behind the rebellion – then rallied support, drove Lothar back to Italy and made a new partition, in which Lothar was passed over in silence. But this time (831) the other two brothers, Pippin and Louis, were dissatisfied, and rebelled. Louis was deposed (833), then restored (835), and each time new dispositions were made. From 829 the reign was simply a struggle of parties, and when Louis died in 840 it was impossible to decide with any certitude which of the numerous acts of succession was legitimate.

The result was further chaos, a struggle among the four sons, issuing finally in the famous treaty of Verdun of 843 – the end of one chapter and the beginning of another. The treaty of Verdun was simply a partition – one son, Pippin, having been set aside – among the three remaining claimants, Lothar, Louis and Charles. Lip-service continued to be paid to the ideal of unity in the shape of a new theory of 'confraternity'; that is, a permanent alliance among the brothers in the interests of the maintenance of peace and of the territorial *status quo*. But it was only lip-service, and 'confraternity' was soon little more than a word. The treaty of Verdun marks, in fact, the burial of the idea of 817 of a united empire – an idea which, in terms of practical politics, was already dead,

68

killed in the civil wars after 829. In so far as the idea of unity survived, it was an ideal unity, of which the church rather than the empire, the papacy rather than the monarchy, was the guardian.

Contemporaries were well aware that the treaty of Verdun marked a climax: Florus of Lyons wrote that henceforward there was no longer an emperor, not even a king, but only 'kinglets', no longer a kingdom but only *fragmina regni*.[21] In fact, his statement is an exaggeration. The imperial title remained, but the attempt to give it substance and meaning had failed; it was, as it had been between 800 and 812, simply a mark of personal pre-eminence, a dignity, a title.[22] Therefore it has been said that the treaty 'substituted for a single empire three independent kingdoms'.[23] But this also is an exaggeration. There had never, in reality, been a single empire, only a policy – abandoned for all practical purposes, as early as 831[24] – of aiming to establish a single empire. All the treaty of Verdun did, therefore, was to recognize 'the coexistence of independent states';[25] it registered the acceptance of what had already happened. Of the three brothers Charles (the son of Louis's second marriage) received the west, Louis (later known as Louis the German) the eastern provinces; the eldest son, Lothar, who already possessed the imperial title, received the belt of country running through the centre, from the mouth of the Rhine down to the mountains of Switzerland and Burgundy, and then south across the Alps to the Mediterranean coast east from the mouth of the Rhône to Italy, and the whole of Lombardy and the Italian province. With the constitution of these three kingdoms a chapter of history was at an end: the Carolingian achievement, the vast territorial bloc which we call the 'empire', had ceased to exist.

But the treaty of Verdun also marked the opening of a new chapter. If it was intended, by means of equitable partition and by the régime of 'confraternity', to bring about a lasting settlement and restore peace, the plan was an almost immediate failure. Not, indeed, that the division was so impracticable as has often been suggested. It is easy, in the light of later events, to suppose that the 'middle' kingdom of Lothar, the 'corridor' (as it has been called) between France and Germany, was destined to be a prey to its two neighbours, that it was a geographical and political monstrosity, with no chance of a 'viable existence',[26] and that the treaty of Verdun simply unleashed wars between east and west, between Germany and France, for control of the 'middle' lands – the consequences of which, it has often been said, 'made themselves felt' from 843 right down to 1945.[27] That is a plausible thesis, but it is not the whole truth. First of all, neither Germany nor France existed in 843; there was, for example, no more unity between the peoples of Brittany and Aquitaine and Burgundy and Neustria in the western kingdom than there was between the mixed populations of Lothar's lands. Secondly, Lothar's share, the 'middle kingdom' as we call it, had advantages of a practical sort. Not only did it contain the two capitals, Rome and Aachen, and was therefore chosen as the emperor's share, but it was also by far the richest of the three divisions and, as the one   69 including within its boundaries the old homeland of the Carolingian dynasty, contained the largest proportion of the royal estates, on which the monarchy depended for its material resources.

With this endowment there was, therefore, no reason why the middle kingdom should not have held, and more than held, its own. In fact Lothar did maintain some sort of balance down to the time of his death, and it was his death in 855, rather than the treaty of Verdun in 843, that was the real turning-point; for Lothar himself had three sons, and now once again, instead of an attempt to maintain unity, there was a further partition, this time of the middle kingdom. The eldest son, Louis, whom Lothar had already made emperor (and who therefore counts as the emperor Louis II) received Italy; the second, Charles, received Provence in the south-west; and the third, Lothar II, received the northern lands which are called (after him, not after his father) Lotharingia or Lorraine.

This partition, unlike that of 843, was really decisive. The empire, which under Lothar had still counted for something, exercising some sort of hegemony over the other two kingdoms, was now confined to Italy, and as a result inevitably fell more and more under the control of the papacy. Louis II is often called simply 'emperor of Italy', a clear indication that the imperial title now implied little more than a claim to rule over Italy, an Italian kingship. Secondly, and more important, the middle kingdom, divided into three separate parts often at loggerheads among themselves, was no longer able to act as a makeweight, or even to hold its own, between the other two. Since Lorraine, as we have seen, was the richest province north of the Alps, with the greatest share of royal estates, it was immediately coveted by the rulers of both east and west. First in the field was the eastern ruler, Louis the German, because the west Frankish king, Charles the Bald, was hampered and tied down at home by unrest and rebellion in Brittany and Aquitaine, where once again, as in the period of Merovingian decadence, the spirit of local independence led to revolts against the Frankish yoke. Thus in 858, only three years after the partition of 855, a first invasion of Lorraine from the east Frankish, or German, kingdom took place.

The invasion of 858 marked the beginning of the long rivalry of east and west, of France and Germany, for Lorraine and the Rhinelands. As it turned out, Louis's attack was a failure; the *status quo* was restored in 860. But in 869, on the death of Lothar II, the two rulers of east and west got together and agreed to partition Lorraine. The agreement in which this deal was registered was the treaty of Meersen (870), and it is important because it brought France and Germany for the first time face to face, in direct contact. But the equality of east and west, which the partition implies, was only momentary. The ceaseless internal difficulties in the west, aggravated now a hundredfold by Danish invasions, crippled the west Frankish (or French) rulers; and after the death of

30 Frankish rulers: king Pippin (upper left), emperor
Charles the Great (upper right), Louis the Pious,
Lothar, Louis the German and Charles the Bald;
from a twelfth-century book cover

Charles the Bald in 877, the predominance of the east Frankish kingdom gave it the whip-hand. The result was that the partition of Lorraine, although confirmed in 878, was revoked, and in 879 the whole of Lorraine passed into the hands of the German ruler.

The same disproportion between the power of the eastern and western Carolingians also affected Italy, where the emperor Louis II had shown himself powerless to combat Saracen invasions. Hence, on his death in 875, the pope looked outside for a candidate who could bring with him some additional resources; and for the last two years of his life, from 875 to 877, Charles the Bald, the west Frankish ruler, was emperor. From then on, however, the relative strength of the German Carolingians prevailed. In 877 the eldest son of Louis the German became Italian ruler, followed in 885 by his brother, Charles the Fat, who ruled as emperor until 887. Thereafter the only question in Italy was whether power, and therewith the royal title and the claim to the imperial title, would fall into the hands of a local Italian family, or whether a German ruler would seize control. The fact that Charles the Fat, who died in 888, was the last legitimate east Frankish Carolingian temporarily weakened the German position; and so from 891 there followed a series of non-Carolingian Italian emperors, Italian noblemen who used their predominance to snatch the imperial title as a means of securing greater authority over their equals. But German intervention in Italy was continuous throughout the period, beginning with the illegitimate Carolingian, Arnulf (896–99), and followed by the dukes of southern Germany, of Swabia and Bavaria. From the beginning of the tenth century the rulers of Provence and Burgundy also intervened; but from 877 the German precedent was set, and once the German or east Frankish monarchy was re-established under a new dynasty after 919, it quickly revived its claims, until finally in 961 Otto I of Germany marched into Italy and seized the imperial throne which had been vacant for forty years.

In intervening in Italy, Otto I was simply following late-Carolingian precedent, the example of Charles the Fat and of Arnulf. The significant point was that this precedent was strong enough to ensure at least that the idea of empire did not disappear completely. Although the Ottonian empire of later times was not a revival of the Carolingian empire, and never established any claim over the west Frankish lands, the connection between the two was forged in the last years of the ninth century. In this way also, therefore, the ninth century was formative: out of it sprang the medieval empire, successor to the Carolingian empire, which perished in bankruptcy and obscurity in 923.[28]

31 Imperial glory: the jewelled head of Charles the Great on a fourteenth-century reliquary

Four   The impact of invasion

SUCH, shorn of complications, and set out as briefly as possible if its complexities are to be intelligible, is the history of the Carolingian empire after the treaty of Verdun in 843. It is a story of collapse and disintegration; and the date of its completion is usually taken to be the deposition of Charles the Fat in December 887 or his death a few weeks later in January 888. The sequel is described in a famous passage in the chronicle of Regino of Prum: 'Then the kingdoms which had been subject to the government of Charles split up into fragments, breaking the bond which united them, and . . . each one sought to create a king of its own, drawn from within itself; which thing was the cause of long wars, not that there were lacking Frankish princes worthy of dominion by their noble birth, their courage and their wisdom, but because their equality in origin and dignity . . . was a fresh cause for discord. None of them was sufficiently raised above the rest to make them willing to submit to his authority.'[1]

In the west, where there was still a legitimate Carolingian line, it was discarded in favour of Odo, count of Paris, who had shown his aptitude in resistance to the Vikings; thenceforward, for a century, down to 987, the west Frankish crown was disputed between the Carolingians and the dynasty of the counts of Paris, until in the end the latter succeeded in winning the throne. In the east, failing a legitimate Carolingian successor, the illegitimate Arnulf was set up as king. Italy was disputed between the two leading dynasties of Carolingian counts, the marquess of Friuli and the marquess of Spoleto. On the Mediterranean seaboard a separate kingdom of Provence was in existence; in Burgundy another kingdom was constituted by Rudolf, great-nephew of the empress Judith (wife of Louis the Pious).

Most of these dynasties were related to the Carolingian line, had Carolingian blood in their veins, and to that extent a Carolingian tradition still persisted. But, as the chronicler wrote, none stood far enough above his fellows in the highest rank of the aristocracy to make his position secure; and their kingdoms were as fragile and unstable as the Carolingian kingdom had already shown itself to be. To suppose that their emergence was the beginning of the independent states of later Europe, would be an illusion. They were one and all temporary group-

32 One of the last surviving remnants of the independent Lombard kingdom: late eighth-century sculpture in Santa Maria in Valle, Cividale

ings, none of which had in it the elements of durability, each destined to collapse before the states of France and Germany and Italy arose from the ruins. There was still, in 887, no France, no Germany, and Italy was only a geographical expression. But the forces from which France and Germany and Italy were born were already there – but under, not upon, the surface.

The kingdoms of 887, as a French historian has rightly pointed out, were 'an illusion, because everywhere life was becoming more and more localized, and at this hour of crumbling the royal crowns had scarcely more concrete value than the imperial diadem'.[2] To see the making of the future we have, therefore, to turn away from the external history of the Carolingian state, and examine its internal transformations. The dissolution of Carolingian unity was important; it opened a way for new forces, broke the old mould and facilitated social regrouping. But the new groupings and new societies that emerged, and in particular the differentiation of social groupings and social forms in the different regions of the Carolingian lands, require further explanation. They were not simply the result of the decline and dissolution of Carolingian society, but that combined with other factors.

VIKINGS, SARACENS AND MAGYARS

Of these factors, by far the most important was the wave of invasions which broke over the Carolingian world in ever-growing intensity in the ninth century.[3] It accompanied, and of course in considerable degree it explains, the failure of the Carolingian rulers. If the Carolingians were displaced in the west in 888, it was because of their failure to cope with the Viking problem; and almost inevitably power passed into and was concentrated in the hands of those who could and did cope. Raids and incursions from outside added materially to the internal difficulties of the Carolingian rulers, and made it increasingly difficult for them to maintain their position. Moreover, the wealth and resources of the monarchies were affected; indeed, the invasions brought a rapid setback to Carolingian society as a whole in the economic sphere. Whereas the early Carolingian period, to 804, had been an age of an expanding economy, after 804 the economy was contracting. Where new land had been brought under the plough, whole areas were now depopulated and returned to nature. In this way not only were royal resources wasted, but political troubles arose, for the aristocracy, seeing its wealth shrinking, began to use its powers to maintain its privileged position, oppressing the poor and plundering the royal demesne.[4] Where previously it had profited best by serving the king, it now saw its profit at the king's expense. Lands assigned for the upkeep of the counts were treated as private possessions and amalgamated with the private property of their holders; in the same way the office of royal commissioner or *missus* was used to bring new territories into subjection.[5]

The general results of the invasions of the ninth century may be summed up as depopulation, agricultural decline, and loss of wealth.

Everywhere also there were empty stomachs, people, uprooted from their homes, seeking a patron who could give them a livelihood and a lord powerful enough to protect them. But the invasions were not one single event. There were invasions from the north, the Viking invasions; invasions from the south, the Saracen invasions; invasions from the east, the Magyars. They were not equal in their impact on the Carolingian lands, and they were not simultaneous. Hence, although they struck the whole of Carolingian Europe with force, they struck some parts more forcibly than others. Therefore, although the general effects were the same, the specific effects varied considerably from region to region.

The Saracen ravages were the longest in duration; but they were the most localized, affecting essentially only the Mediterranean seaboard. Moreover, they were really only piratical raids, and the raiders rarely settled down to a systematic siege. Since the area they threatened was the old home of the Roman city, Provence and Lombardy and Italy, this is of importance; it means that they affected only the countryside and had little effect on town life. Consequently the towns of Italy continued to develop, and in some ways their development was accentuated by the fact that they were centres of resistance to the raiders.

Much the same is true of the Magyars, appearing as bands of swift-moving horsemen, who rarely attempted a siege; the only fortified place they are known to have taken was Pavia in Lombardy. Nevertheless the Magyar invasions were far more important in their effects than the Saracen raids, for the brunt of their attack fell on Germany, where there were few fortified towns, and the open countryside was desolated. They had an easy field of action, because the eastern policy of Charles the Great, his destruction of an independent Saxony in the north-east, and still more the destruction of the Avar kingdom in the south-east, meant the end of the two powers which might have provided a bulwark of resistance. But the Magyars came late on the scene, and the period of their attacks was therefore limited. Their first appearance in Germany was in 862; but they did not become a serious menace until the very end of the century. They attacked Bavaria in 900 and Saxony in 906; in 899 they appeared in Italy in the valley of the Po, and in 917 they broke through via Italy to Burgundy and Provence. Thereafter their raids became more and more infrequent; and their final defeat by Otto I, at the battle of the Lech, occurred in 955. For some time before that, however, they had gradually been settling down to a sedentary life on the Danube, where they were forming the Hungarian state; and this process was helped forward by their conversion to Christianity through the efforts of bishop Pilgrim of Passau (971–91). Under St Stephen, at the beginning of the eleventh century, Hungary became an established state, and the Magyar incursions into western Europe ceased.

Far more tenacious than either Magyars or Saracens were the Vikings. Compared with the former, their attacks were also far more extended in time. As we have seen, Viking raids had already troubled the last years of Charlemagne himself. A generation later they began wintering in the lands they were attacking: in Ireland in 835, in France in 843, in England in 851. Thenceforward it was no longer a case of sporadic raids, but of planned and methodical attack, in which they systematically set out to gain control of the urban centres; and we know of many important towns – Cologne, Rouen, Nantes, Orléans, Bordeaux, London, York – which had already succumbed by 888. The raids, as this list shows, were widespread at first. Lorraine, the Rhinelands and the northern parts of Germany suffered from Norman incursions, as well as France. But from about 885 the Danes concentrated their attention on the valleys of the Loire and the Seine, tending more and more to leave the waters of the Rhine and the Scheldt; and in 896 a permanent settlement was begun on the lower reaches of the Seine – a settlement which was the core of the future duchy of Normandy. Partly as a result of this territorial acquisition which absorbed new Viking settlers, partly in consequence of the consolidation and stabilization of the Scandinavian kingdoms, the first phase of Viking expansion ceased; and when a second phase began, a century later, in the time of Canute the Great (1016–35), it was different in character; it had ceased to be sporadic raiding and became systematic conquest directed by strong kings for political purposes – an aggressive foreign policy which reached its peak in Canute's imperialism.

One of the most serious features of these three waves of invasion, Magyar, Saracen and Scandinavian, for the Carolingian lands was that they were simultaneous, so that in the second half of the ninth century Carolingian Europe was threatened on all sides at once. But of the three, the Danish invasions were most persistent and most serious; and there is no doubt that the western half of the kingdom suffered worst of all, particularly since, as the Frankish homeland, furthest removed from the frontiers, it was worst prepared for defence. In the outlying regions of his empire, Charles the Great had organized marches for the express purpose of holding off incursions and ravages; and this marcher organization was better able to stand the strain than the county organization of Gaul. Consequently in France, more than elsewhere, the invasions meant a new beginning: the building of ramparts and fortifications, and away from the towns the construction of castles and earthworks. The effects of the invasions were not, therefore, the same everywhere, but varied in accordance with conditions in the different parts of Europe.

REGIONAL DIVERSITY

Carolingian government was far less uniform than is often supposed; and the impact of invasion, falling on different regions in different intensity, emphasized the divergencies. All along the eastern frontiers of Germany, as well as on the march of Spain and in Italy both on the eastern frontier of Lombardy and in the south on the Byzantine border, were dukes or marquesses with powers more extensive than those of counts.[6] But even further inland divergencies were considerable. Bavaria, for example, after its conquest in 788, had been placed under a governor-general, a close relative of Charles himself; in Saxony the

33 A runic stone commemorating a Viking's three expeditions to England

position was similar.[7] Aquitaine in the south-west was constituted a kingdom as early as 781. It was, in fact, only in the old homeland, the core of the Frankish dominions, where the organization of counties already had a long history and· was indigenous in the land, that there were no intermediate grades, 'prefects', dukes or margraves.[8]

These differences alone were sufficient, under the stress of invasion, to produce very different results. Furthermore, it must be borne in mind that the Carolingian empire was not a homogeneous state with a single political tradition, but a series of conquests held together only by the common factor of Frankish rule, and with many underlying differences. So long as Frankish expansion continued, these differences were veiled; it seemed as though the administration imposed on the conquered lands in the Frankish interest had succeeded in binding them together in a common network of government. But, when the uniform administrative machinery broke down as a result of the civil wars, the long-standing historical differences reasserted themselves.

The wars under Louis the Pious and the series of partitions that followed were fatal to the Carolingian administration. Civil strife and conflicting claims undermined the loyalty of the small body of royal vassals, on whose willing services its functioning had all along depended. When none could tell which of the many pretendants, all claiming to be the true king, was the legitimate ruler, when loyal service to one pretendant was treated by another as treason, the whole moral basis of government was sapped. Moreover, the partitions destroyed the unity of this governing class, which sprang (as we have seen) almost without exception from a small number of associated families, stemming from the Carolingian patrimony in the lower Rhineland and along the Meuse, but which were now – if seated, for example, in Italy – separated from their homeland by artificial frontiers. Inevitably, in these circumstances, local representatives of Carolingian power concentrated on making themselves so strong that they could hold their own against any of the pretendants; and inevitably this meant concentration on their own local interests. Thus the main administrative link of unity snapped; and the tendency to local concentration was reinforced by the invasions, in which each locality looked after itself as best it could.

In this way the underlying regional differences, both of organization and of history, which had been temporarily suppressed in the time of Charles the Great, once again came into the foreground, and became more and more the dominant factors. Carolingian government had never succeeded in abolishing them; it had only driven them under the surface of a superficial uniformity which ceased to exist once the royal vassals, the *vassi dominici*, ceased to function in the interests of the monarchy. Under the stress of invasion the long-standing differences re-emerged, and from then on they were the deciding influence, transforming the Carolingian world into a series of distinct and separate societies.

These differences were embodied, essentially, in the different histories of the lands which had been absorbed into the Carolingian dominions. To consider them in detail would require a review of the history of western Europe from the time of the barbarian invasions in the fifth century; but it is important to realize how far-reaching they were. The Frankish dominions comprised peoples at very different levels of culture, and the different provinces came under Frankish rule or were affected by Frankish influences for widely different periods of time. Some provinces, such as Burgundy or Aquitaine, although they had ancient cultures of their own, had long been penetrated by Frankish civilization and Frankish institutions, although they had made use of successive weakenings of Frankish power to revert to a more autonomous position. Others, such as Lombardy and Saxony, came under Frankish control only in the reign of Charlemagne himself. Yet Lombardy and Saxony were very different in status and history, and set very different problems for the Frankish government. In Lombardy the Franks had come face to face with a civilization to all intents and purposes as far developed as their own; in Saxony, they had to deal with a people which had not yet reached the stage of monarchical government, which had never experienced Roman rule, and which at the time of Charles the Great's conquest had not yet been converted to Christianity. Very important, again, was the persistence of city life in Italy, which – unlike the Frankish conquest of

34 A Saxon casket with elements of Christian iconography; presumably early ninth century

Gaul – the Lombard conquest had not disturbed; it contrasts very markedly with Germany where – except in the Rhineland, and even there on nothing like the same scale as in Italy – there was very little municipal life. It also contrasts with Gaul north of the Loire, where the importance of the cities had shrunk to nothing and society was essentially agrarian.

Evidently, such differences affected the character of government, whether the Franks desired it or not; and the superficial uniformity of the Frankish county system only hid, but did not abolish these differences. In point of fact, it simply had not enough time to do so; the period between its introduction in Saxony (for example) or in Lombardy and the decline under Louis the Pious was far too short. It was only in the old Frankish core of the Carolingian lands that the institution of the count and the county was rooted in the countryside, reaching back with a continuous history to the days of Clovis. There – but there alone – through the sheer attrition of time, the counts had displaced the old popularly elected officers of local self-government, or reduced them to strict dependence as their deputies, and had become the pivot of local administration. Elsewhere, as we have seen, the Frankish count was in essence the agent of the Frankish kings, sent out to supervise the conquered lands in the interests of the Frankish monarchy; and under him the old local institutions of the conquered peoples remained in existence as the effective means of local government. Once the civil wars and then the invasions weakened the position of the count, it is comprehensible enough that the older institutions, submerged but not displaced, once 81 again resumed their original role. Institutions, it has been said, which 'depended chiefly upon local organization or ingrained custom . . . had hardy roots'; but 'devices which are predicated upon political stability, which are motivated by the idea that the preservation of public order is the business of the ruler . . . display less capacity to maintain themselves in the face of adverse circumstances.'[9]

THE DISINTEGRATION OF THE CAROLINGIAN WORLD

Once these elementary but basic facts are understood, it is evident that what was important for the future was not the superficial uniformity of government superimposed by the Carolingians, but the more profound internal divergencies and differences which persisted throughout Carolingian times under the surface. Partly because the impact of the invasions was different in intensity in different regions, but first and foremost because each province in the Frankish empire had a character of its own, each region reacted in its own way to the common problems which the invasions created; and in each case the reaction was conditioned by factors which reached back to pre-Carolingian times. The invasions were the solvent; thereafter the different provinces went their own way. That, fundamentally, is why it is impossible, after 843, to deal with Carolingian Europe as a whole, and why the history of the Carolingian empire after that time, the history of the rulers and their relations between themselves and with the pope, their treaties and their wars, is only part of the story, and by no means its most important part. The fundamental changes in social structure, which would count in the future, were taking place in the different provinces, independent of the will and actions of the rulers, whose activities, therefore, unable as they were to arrest or even to direct the course of events, became increasingly insignificant and meaningless in the historical process.

At this point, therefore, it is necessary to turn away from the general history of the Carolingian empire as a whole, and deal with the separate histories of the different regions. These are of fundamental importance; for their history is the history of the formation of the medieval – and, indeed, of the modern – European states, and of the distinctive institutions which differentiate them. As yet, of course, these states did not exist; there was in 843, or even in 888, no France, no Germany, no Italy. The states created by the various partitions were, as a French historian has said, 'an illusion'; they had no durability.[10] The old view, often repeated, that the Carolingian empire 'broke up' into 'partition-states', that all that happened in the ninth century was a division of the Carolingian empire, is false and misleading. In reality the process of disintegration went much further. The kingdoms which arose in the following two hundred years were not the direct successors of the Carolingian state, but were born of the anarchy resulting from the dissolution of the Carolingian state; and if it is true that there is no coherent history of the Carolingian empire in this period, it is also true that there is no coherent

82 history of the kingdoms – France, Italy, Germany and Burgundy –

which began, in this period, to take shape.

There was certainly nothing preordained about the rise of any of these kingdoms. Until 955, for example, there was no guarantee of the emergence of a Germany, such as we recognize, even as a mere territorial unit. For years there was a possibility of north and south Germany going their own ways as separate lands; and for years also there was a possibility – perhaps even a likelihood – of the junction of Swabia and Lorraine and Burgundy to form a massive central kingdom which, by depriving Germany of its western provinces, would have altered the whole physiognomy of the German state, just as it would have absorbed lands later French.

These are only some of the possibilities in the historical situation at the end of the ninth and the beginning of the tenth centuries; further west, the situation was at least as complex and uncertain. When we talk of France and Germany and Italy, therefore, we are using terms which are essentially our own, making a simplification which suits our purposes, but which does not accurately reflect the true position. The reality is that political life, for the whole of this period, was being concentrated more and more in different provinces, regions, duchies, counties; and the history of no two was identical. It was only gradually, at very different speeds in different lands, that from these provinces larger units, kingdoms, took shape; and then with no logic or compelling force. Hence the history – the history that matters – of the two centuries after 843 is immensely complex. It is difficult, if not impossible, to find generalizations valid for all areas of modern France or of modern Germany. Nevertheless, with our eye on the future and our knowledge of what was going to come about, we can pick out a number of differentiating features; and to these we shall now turn, taking one by one the areas which later were to become France and Germany and Italy, and seeing how the separate states evolved, what the characteristic institutions of each were, and why and how their history was so different, in spite of the fact that all had belonged to the Carolingian state. The reaction of Anglo-Saxon England to the Viking invasions was also distinctive, and contrasted markedly with that on the continent.

Five   Feudal France: origins

IT IS USEFUL to start with the west Frankish kingdom – that is, with the lands later to be known as France – partly because France was the core of the Frankish dominions, and partly because it was in France that the effects of the invasions were longest lived and most severe. In the west Frankish lands the invasions initiated a long period – in which the transference of royal power from the Carolingian dynasty to the Capetian dynasty marks no break – running roughly from 850 to 1050 or 1060 and perhaps beyond. In other words, it took more than two centuries before a new society with a recognizable shape or outline arose from the anarchy produced by the invasions; and it was only in the eleventh century that the twin processes of territorial regrouping and social reclassification were completed. Prior to that, there is no firm outline, and it is practically impossible to trace a fixed line of historical development, unless we turn to the individual histories of particular counties and localities. That was where the real process of reshaping took place from which eventually the map of feudal France would emerge.

By comparison, the history of the kings is utterly insignificant. Only with the accession of Louis VI in the year 1100 does the monarchy begin to count; the history of the first four Capetians is even more insignificant than that of the last Carolingians, who had at any rate a relic of great traditions behind them. Down to 1100 the history of France is the history of the feudal dynasties, not of the royal dynasty. There was no settled government, no organized state. We can see at play the raw forces which, later, would be harnessed in a constitution; but no constitution existed. The consequences of the invasions for the west Frankish lands were, in short, a fractioning of public powers, which continued beyond the end of the tenth century; and when, later, they were slowly and painfully reconstituted, it was on a new basis. It was not, therefore, merely a question of a change in the balance of power within the state, a transference of royal powers into the hands of counts and other local magnates, a realignment in the relations of local and central authority. On the contrary, the whole existing framework of government was rent asunder, and in its place there appeared something new. If we wish to summarize the change, we may say that the Carolingian state, with its

35 Presentation of a bible to Charles the Bald by count Vivian, the lay abbot of St Martin of Tours

proto-feudal features, gave way to a state in which feudalism was the only effective force.

THE FEUDALIZATION OF FRENCH SOCIETY

The change was at once social and political; and, of course, the two aspects of the transformation went on simultaneously, affected each other and were closely interconnected. For the purposes of discussion, however, it is convenient to separate them, and to take the underlying social changes first.[1]

These are, in general terms, obvious enough and easy to understand. The invasions, basically, did two things: they created an overwhelming need for protection, which the monarchy was unable to provide, and they put a premium on knighthood, on the ability to bear arms, to fight, to ward off attack. Before the Viking threat the monarchy capitulated in the west Frankish kingdom as elsewhere, seeking in vain to buy off the raiders by payments of Danegeld, which only made them more avaricious, or diverting them by letting them loose against provinces which did not recognize the king's authority. The first ruler in the west Frankish kingdom to pay Danegeld was Charles the Bald in 845; and his long reign (840–77) was crucial for the future. Under him each province, each county, each valley, almost each village, was thrown back upon self-defence. The result was the building of earthworks and castles, which became the symbol of feudal society. The castle, and only the castle, provided protection – at a price. And the price was subordination, subjection, dependence. But, the circumstances being what they were, it was willingly paid. Freedom meant freedom to starve, to be pillaged and murdered; it was gladly surrendered for the protection which a strong man could provide for his dependants.

The result was the rapid obliteration of the small free peasant proprietors, whom the Carolingians, particularly Charles the Great, had made efforts to protect and foster, and the reduction of French society, in the course of three or four generations – a century or thereabouts – to two classes only. On the one side, there was the numerous class of servile dependants, who had lost their personal freedom, and who had henceforward no political importance, who answered simply to their immediate lord, and with whom government had no concern. On the other side, there was the class which is indiscriminately known as *liber*, *ingenuus*, *nobilis*, the noble class, in which all political rights were vested, and which had engrossed for itself all the rights which, in earlier Frankish society, had belonged to the far wider class of freemen, including peasant freemen. After the end of the ninth century, there was, in France, no free class considerable enough in numbers to matter politically which was not noble. The free man was noble, and the nobleman was free – the terms were equivalent – and the free (non-noble) peasantry of the Carolingian epoch had disappeared. To be a peasant, to live by cultivating the soil, meant to be servile. No freeman could live by cultivating the soil, and no unfree tenant was fit for the profession of arms: this difference alone established a fixed division between the classes.

But the events which resulted in the depression of the peasantry to a uniform servile status – a depression from which they began to recover only at the end of the twelfth and in the thirteenth century – also changed the character of the noble class. The criterion was no longer birth, noble blood, or even royal service, but ability to bear arms. The invasions, in other words, put military service so much in the forefront among the duties of the vassal, that military service, the profession of arms, became the sole criterion of nobility. All engaged in the profession of arms, whatever their wealth and position, were noble; and all were in this degree equal. The change was no less fundamental than that which took place in the status of the peasantry; for it meant that vassalage lost any stigma of dependence, that the relationship of vassalage could be entered into without degradation, that a member of the nobility could become a vassal without losing caste. Consequently, vassalage – which, in origin, had contained elements of servitude, service in return for land – was 'ennobled' and became the typical relationship of the higher ranks of French society.

Time and time again, almost without exception, the same man was lord and vassal; and the result was the growth of a sense of social equality and solidarity within the noble class. Because a lord was so often someone else's vassal, he had no interest in depressing the rights of vassalage; because a vassal was himself lord over others, he had every interest in maintaining the rights of lordship. In France, therefore, vassalage, although it meant dependence on another, did not imply subordination, but denoted 'freedom' or 'nobility' – it was a relationship into which only a 'free' or 'noble' man might enter – and so, from the anarchy produced by the Viking invasions, a new free class emerged, a class which was at one and the same time free and noble, and which claimed its freedom and nobility because it could devote itself entirely to the profession of arms. Thus France saw, in the ninth and tenth centuries, a profound social revolution, the creation of a new society, long before such a social revolution was completed elsewhere; and this revolution was inevitably accompanied and reflected by related changes in the political structure, which was gradually adapted to suit the new circumstances and the new social environment.

The political changes, the changes in the character of French government, which occurred in the two centuries beginning about 850, have frequently been described as the replacement of the Carolingian official hierarchy by a feudal hierarchy, and the 'appropriation' or 'usurpation' of royal powers by local magnates. Neither statement is accurate, nor do they adequately describe what took place. To speak of the replacement of an official by a feudal hierarchy overlooks the fact that feudalism, the relationship of man to man, the reliance of the lord on his vassals, and particularly the reliance of the king on the royal vassals, already played a great part in Charles the Great's government. Nevertheless, it was never the whole of Charles's government. There was still a free population, 87 looking directly to the king, without intermediate lords, as their ruler; and consequently the disappearance of the non-noble free classes, and their reduction to serfdom, was of fundamental importance. It left the king, so to speak, without subjects, except for the great lords who held their lands of him as his vassals, and except for the tenants on the royal demesnes. But the civil wars of the ninth century, and the consequent need to buy support by concessions of land, resulted in an almost total dispersion of the royal estates, which meant that the king had few dependants and also – since land was the source of wealth – little revenue. By the time the Carolingians were superseded by the Capetians in 987 practically nothing was left, and the Capetians themselves, who had been competing for the throne for the best part of a century, and had also had to recompense their supporters, were little better off. That, without doubt, is the basic explanation of the insignificance of both dynasties down to the end of the eleventh century: their landed properties and material wealth were far smaller than those of many of the princes.

The decline of the 'fisc', the squandering of the royal estates, was therefore the second reason for the decline of the monarchy. It meant also that the monarch was unable to retain the services of the vassals on whom, as we have seen, Charles the Great had depended for the execution of government. Nothing, perhaps, is more significant than the disappearance of the *vassi dominici*, who in Charles the Great's time had represented the king's interests throughout the realm. They are last mentioned in a charter of 943;[2] and although it is possible that a few later instances may be discovered, the date is noteworthy enough. The Normans first wintered in France in 843; the charter is dated 943. Within a century of the invasions, therefore, the *vassi dominici*, who had been the backbone of Carolingian government, had disappeared from the scene.

Abbot Odo of Cluny, in his life of count Gerald of Aurillac, throws light upon the process by which they were engulfed. 'Owing', he says, 'to the disturbed state of the realm, the marquises made immoderate demands on the royal vassals and reduced them to dependence.'[3] Thus Gerald himself was asked by duke William of Aquitaine 'to leave the royal service and commend himself' to the duke. Gerald, however, was an exception and refused; but his nephew, Rainald, commended himself to William 'with a huge number of knights'. Of the two, without doubt, the nephew was the more typical figure. The tenth century saw the *vassi dominici* cease to be *vassi dominici*, and become instead not vassals of the king but vassals of the great feudatories. Thus in the end, apart from the vassals on the few remaining royal estates, only the great feudal princes remained direct or 'immediate' vassals of the crown. All other vassals were 'mediatized', i.e. subjected to the princes, and so were removed from direct contact with the monarchy. Once this process was completed, the old Carolingian constitution, of which the *vassi dominici* had been the main pillar, was dead.

To speak of this process as 'usurpation' or 'appropriation' of royal powers by the great princes is not adequate. The growing feudalization

36 A French lord hawking; detail from a twelfth-century decorated chest

of society was not resisted by the monarchy,[4] because it perceived that the powers of the feudal lord were a force which could be used as a means of bolstering up law and order, by making the lord responsible for his men. It was carried out not against, but in co-operation with, the royal government, which was forced by circumstances to place greater powers in the hands of the local potentates, as a means of meeting the gathering danger from beyond the frontiers.

This change of policy can be observed already in the reign of Louis the Pious and was continued by his successor, Charles the Bald. It is seen in the increased independence which was now allowed to the duchies of Aquitaine, Brittany and Provence, and to the counties of Toulouse and Barcelona. And it is seen, more strikingly, in the creation in the interior of the land of similar higher territorial commands; thus, for example, the duchy 'between Seine and Loire', which fell into the hands of the count of Paris, the founder of the Capetian dynasty; thus, again, the duchy of Maine; thus, also, Flanders, where the counts of Bruges, as the strongest local potentates most likely to lead the resistance to the Northmen, were granted some other counties, including Ghent and Courtrai, by Charles the Bald in about the year 863.[5]

It is important to realize that the crown itself tacitly admitted and in some cases consciously sponsored this movement of local concentration; that it was not due simply to the insubordination of the nobility. But greater local independence, although it was a factor favouring feudalism, was not necessarily the same thing as feudalism; and it was somewhat 89 later – not under Louis the Pious, when decentralization began, but under his son, Charles the Bald – that feudalism was accepted by the crown, and feudal practices were sanctioned as the only means of preserving order and maintaining some remnant of social organization. Three famous capitularies issued by Charles mark this change, and each is worth a few words of explanation and discussion:

1 In the capitulary of Meersen (847) Charles ordered all free men to choose a lord, and likewise forbade them to leave their lord without just reason.

2 The second, issued at Thionville, gave official recognition to the vassal's oath.

3 At Kiersy (877), in the most famous of all his capitularies, Charles sanctioned hereditary succession to counties and other fiefs.

Historians have rightly warned us not to exaggerate the significance of these texts. None, probably, was intended as a permanent measure; none was without precedent in the past, and the capitulary of Kiersy merely gave formal recognition to a practice which had developed earlier. Furthermore, it is quite certain that the capitulary of Meersen was not applied systematically; after 847 and for another century, there were still plenty of men without a lord.[6] Nevertheless, the importance of these capitularies still remains considerable; for now for the first time what had been tendencies were expressed in precise legal form.[7] The crown was never again in the position to revoke its acts; and so, like many things intended to be temporary, the capitularies set a precedent.

In each case, moreover, a fundamental point was at issue. If a man was forbidden to leave his lord without just cause, that meant in fact that the bond of vassalage was made permanent in all normal cases; while by ordering men who had no lord to choose one, the king recognized the normality of feudal relationships. Secondly, in regard to the vassal's oath, the change of emphasis by comparison with Charles the Great was marked. Charles, in 789 and 802, had revived the general oath of fealty, which had fallen into disuse at the end of the seventh century, and imposed it on all free men.[8] Now this oath of fealty, which bound all free men to the king, without feudal intermediaries, fell into oblivion, and was displaced by the more binding and potent oath of homage. Vassalage thus became the only bond between lord and man, between king and people; and the king's only contact with the free population was through a long chain of oaths of homage, owed by one man to another, and on to the next and to the next, and only finally to the king.

But the capitulary of Kiersy was the act which set the seal on the developments that had occurred between 843 and 877. Even in the second half of the ninth century, when the principle of hereditary succession was gathering force, there are plenty of instances to show that it was not the rule.[9] After 877 it became fixed, and therewith the king's hands were tied; he could only deprive a family of its rights if it committed a specific offence against feudal law; otherwise he had no control over the personnel of the counts, and the county administration therewith passed out of his hands. The counties were held, like any other fief, by hereditary right, their transmission governed by feudal law; they had ceased to be part of the royal machinery of government.

THE NEW SUZERAINS

In the political history of the west Frankish lands, the feudalization of the counties is the capital fact; for the county was, throughout this area, the basis of the new, feudal order which slowly and with many setbacks arose out of the ruins of the Carolingian state. The reasons for this are not difficult to explain. In France alone was the county an institution which extended back for centuries before Charles the Great. Hence, when the invasions began, and with them the disorganization of government, the county remained as the stable element. Not, indeed, exclusively, but certainly normally, it was round the person of the count or of the viscount that the new feudal groupings were formed, because he was the outstanding local leader, firmly established in his county, and not – as in Germany or Italy – merely a foreign superintendent sent in to watch over the interests of the monarchy.

In France, therefore, it was mainly the counts who profited from the growth of feudalism; they were the obvious persons to turn to for protection. So we find that the suitors in the county courts, the *scabini*, became the count's vassals, and in this way the public courts became vassals' courts; in short, justice was feudalized. The county, in France, was the starting-point from which development began on the morrow of the ninth-century invasions; and for that reason we can say that the organization of medieval France sprang – in a way which (as we shall see) was not true in Germany and Italy – from its organization in Carolingian times. Precisely because it was not merely a creation of the Carolingians but an ancient institution of the Frankish people, the county, in France, stood firm through the anarchy produced by the invasions. Its shape was changed; it was modified and then reassembled; it was feudalized; but it was not swept away. The feudal principality was the outcome; the Carolingian county was the starting-point. From the time of the invasions it was certain that reconstruction would be on the basis of feudalism, that the map of eleventh-century France would be a feudal map, and that the county would be the foundation from which the new order was to spring.

On the other hand, there was no saying, in advance, what the actual feudal map was going to be. That was due to political circumstances, over which there was no control, and was largely fortuitous. There was no predicting which of the comital families would rise above the other counts, and turn its county into a principality. The reason for this, essentially, is that, owing to the conditions prevalent in the western parts of the Frankish lands, there were no families picked out for leadership. Historians at one time held that the principalities of eleventh-century France were a recrudescence, owing to the breakdown of

Carolingian government in the anarchy of invasion, of the pre-Frankish territorial divisions of Gaul; a resurgence of the 'suppressed nationalities', which – in Aquitaine, for example, or in Burgundy – the Franks had conquered; and in this view the feudal principalities represented racial or ethnic groupings, and the princes rose to power as the leaders of these groups.[10] But this view is no longer prevalent.[11] No one would deny the reality of regional divergencies; but they were not – even in Brittany, for example, which had always remained distinct in speech and otherwise – a decisive political factor. And the reason, basically, was that the county organization, in the west, had taken too firm a hold.

West Frankish society at the beginning of the ninth century was, in its upper ranks, essentially a society of equals; among the counts there were no 'natural' superiors. And it was from this society that the future princes arose. They were simply 'feudatories like the others, who managed, through energy or intelligence, to impose their suzerainty on a certain number of other counts or barons, without reference to ethnographic considerations of any sort'.[12] One factor alone may have helped certain families to prevail over the others, and that was the grants of additional powers which, as we have seen, were made to certain families in threatened areas during the reigns of Louis the Pious and his son, Charles the Bald. This seems, for example, to have been the basis – but only the basis – of the power of the later counts of Flanders. But in general, the process of differentiation took the form of a struggle of all against all, in which energy, brute force, and personality were the factors at play. For this reason personalities counted in this age more than institutions, and in practically every region of France we find in the tenth century personalities whose names stand out high above those of the kings of the period: Richard 'le Justicier' in Burgundy, Herbert of Vermandois in Champagne, William the Pious in Aquitaine, Arnold I in Flanders, and Alan I in Brittany. It was to these men, rather than to the kings, Carolingian and Capetian alike, that the reconstruction of France as a feudal state was due.[13]

To trace their work would mean following, district by district, the evolution of the map of feudal France; and that is a task which can only be accomplished in the detailed framework of local history.[14] But one generalization stands out: namely, that everywhere reconstruction was a process of piecemeal building from the bottom upwards. That is why we have to beware of thinking of the Carolingian state breaking up into coherent duchies and large principalities. The beginnings were much smaller. Thus the later dukes of Aquitaine were not dukes to begin with: they began simply as counts of Poitiers, and then gradually built up a duchy for themselves by extending their authority, in a slow process of consolidation, over the rival comital and viscomital families of their region: Saintonge, Angoulême, La Marche, Limoges. In Flanders, in the same way, the later ruling family started as counts of Bruges, turned the powers given it for the struggle with the Vikings against the other local families, and extended its authority into Artois and over the counties of Thérouanne and Tournai. 'Very few', writes the monkish chronicler of Flanders, 'managed to escape the domination of the feudal prince and to remain solely responsible to the royal authority.'

The story of Burgundy is substantially the same. The first of the line of the later dukes of Burgundy was Richard 'le Justicier', who was simply count of Autun; but, taking upon himself the task of organizing resistance to the Viking invaders, he extended his sphere of power, adding county after county to his lands, and forcing the comital families of the region, who had been his equals, to become his vassals and subordinates. In 894 he secured the county of Sens, in 900 he became count of Auxerre, and one by one the other counts of the region – Troyes, Dijon, Nevers, Chalon-sur-Saône – together with the bishop of Langres, appeared among his vassals. Just as the counts of Poitiers called themselves dukes of Aquitaine, so in Richard's case his title of duke or marquis or even 'prince' of Burgundy was a title which he took to mark his predominant position; it was not a rank or honour – still less a function – created and conferred by the crown.

Other instances may be enumerated more rapidly. The dukes of Brittany, originally counts of Rennes, established their predominance, and therewith their claim to the ducal title, only after long and bitter struggles with the rival family of the counts of Nantes. The counts of Champagne – whose sphere of power was entirely equal to that of others who called themselves duke, although they kept the title of count – rose gradually from being counts of Troyes. And other families, equally important in feudal France, had even smaller beginnings. The powerful family of the counts of Blois, who accumulated no fewer than eight important counties, began simply as viscounts of Tours; that, as late as 999, is the title of the earliest member of the family known to us. And in the same way the counts of Anjou, from whom the Plantagenet kings of England descended, had originally been viscounts of Angers, and had only usurped the title of count when – particularly in the time of the famous Fulk Nerra – they extended their power over the eastern regions of Touraine.

The methods by which these families established their predominance amounted, in sum, to little more than force. They showed, when it suited them, a sovereign disregard for the supposed principles of feudal law – for example, in regard to hereditary succession – which the higher feudatories, the princes, forced the king to respect where they themselves were concerned. The history of one fief in Anjou between 987 and 1060 shows that, of five men to whom it was granted by the two counts, Fulk Nerra and Geoffrey Martel, only two were blood-relations.[15] Notable also was the remorseless pressure on all free landholders, who had 'allodial' lands, to hand over their properties and receive them back, in return for homage, as fiefs; and this particularly if the proprietor had built himself a castle, for his defence and security, on his 'allod'. The history of Flanders and of Hainault is really the history of the reduction, one by one, of the independent castles to the status of fiefs, held of the   93 counts.[16] And once the castles had been acquired, there was a tendency visible – at all events in the eleventh century, if not earlier – not to hand them out again as fiefs, but to confide them to 'captains' or 'castellans', who held them on the count's behalf, and often to make them into centres of administrative districts, known as 'castellanies', for the collection of dues.[17]

Thus gradually, and with many setbacks, the outline of an ordered administration comes into sight. And it is a very important fact, in French history, that this process of territorial consolidation did not stop at the laity, but also embraced the church. As we have seen, the duke of Burgundy forced the bishop of Langres to become his vassal; and this is but one example of a general process. A French chronicler, writing of the period of Hugh Capet, says: 'The duke of Aquitaine and the other magnates of the realm began to acquire that power over the bishops, which hitherto the kings had possessed.' The result was that the monarchy lost that direct connection with the church which had been so great a source of strength to the Carolingians; it lost its ability to place royal nominees in the majority of monasteries and episcopal sees, and thus to use them and their lands and resources as a pillar of royal power. Of a total of seventy-seven French bishoprics, in the end no more than twenty-five remained under royal control. In the case of the monasteries, feudal control was even more far-reaching; and it is no accident that it is in France alone that we hear of the *feudum presbyterale* – that the ordinary ecclesiastical benefice, in other words, was turned into a fief owing homage and service. Thus the clergy, like the lay nobility, were subjected to feudal bonds. The churches of the land were brought within the feudal hierarchy, and feudalism became the dominant principle in every sphere of life.

KING AND PRINCES

Considered in detail, this whole process was extraordinarily complicated and extraordinarily halting. It did not get under way, as a steady process of feudal reconstruction, on the morrow of the invasions. To begin with, and for more than one generation, the trend was not towards reconstruction but towards further fractioning; and many of the factors which had brought about the dissolution of the power of the Carolingians and favoured the princes, affected the princes and weakened their position as well. As we have seen, the Capetians had already lost the greater part of their lands long before the change of dynasty in 987;[18] and this fractioning of power went on until the end of the tenth century. At the end of the ninth century we can count twenty-nine separate territories within France; by the end of the tenth century, the number had risen to fifty-five; and it was only then that the process of concentration and reconstruction got seriously under way.

The outcome was a political and social system totally different from that of Carolingian times. The kingship remained; it made no formal surrender of any of the powers exercised by the Carolingian rulers. But

37 A count performing the traditional act of homage to a bishop; from a twelfth-century Spanish manuscript

it lost its substance, was unable to exercise its inherited royal functions, and right down to the end of the eleventh century played no part in the process of feudal reconstruction. Feudal France was the creation of the princes, not indeed against the crown, or even in opposition to the crown, but without the crown's participation. And the king, in general, accepted this position. Formally, he did not cease to be sovereign, because no one challenged his sovereignty, which he was in no position to make effective; but in practice he was suzerain, and content to be just that. 95

The clearest sign of the change in the king's position is the cessation of royal activities affecting the kingdom as a whole. Within a few years of the death of Charles the Bald in 877, no more capitularies were issued; it was, in fact, impossible for the king, who had no foothold outside his demesne-lands, to legislate for the kingdom as a whole. The royal demesne was administered by the early Capetians as a fief, in exactly the same way as the fiefs of the great princes were administered. The general oath of fealty, as we have seen, disappeared early. Henceforward the king, outside his own demesne, had contact only with the great princes, and it was the princes who ruled – that is to say, who controlled the feudatories within their principalities. The inhabitants of the principalities were responsible, owed duties, only to their princely lords. And this state of affairs was accepted by the king. For him his kingdom was no longer something which he directly administered, but what in French is called the *mouvance* – i.e., the collection of great fiefs which 'move' or are held in chief of the king. The outcome was the gradual formation of a feudal pyramid.

In this pyramid, it is important to note, the king had his place.[19] He was the summit, the apex; he was in fact the keystone which held it together, and there was never any suggestion that the pyramid could do without the king. In that respect his position as suzerain of suzerains was secure, and the kingship was a great deal more than an empty title. On the other hand, since in fact the king's only contact was with a score or more of great princes, whose landed power and resources were at least equal to his own; since at most he could play off the one against the other and so secure his position by holding a balance; and since he could only govern through them, and in fact regarded it as right and proper that he should govern through them, the contractual element in his position became self-evident. The sense of the monarchy as something divinely ordained, towering above all other earthly institutions, which had been a source of strength to the Carolingians in the eighth century, withered. The king's power was now regarded as conditional; that is to say, if the subject, even the greatest, had duties to the king, so the king had duties to his subjects – that is, to the only subjects who counted politically, the princes – and the loyalty of the subjects – that is, the magnates – to the king was subject to his loyalty to them.

This attitude to the monarchy was not, of course, entirely new. Charles the Great, for example, on his first expedition to Italy, had not dared to cross the Alps until he had secured the express assent of his 'faithful'.[20] But it was vastly strengthened in the struggles of the ninth century, and was reinforced still more by the prevalence of the idea of the feudal contract. A document issued under Charles the Bald in 856 best expresses the change: 'Be it known', it is there said, 'that the king has joined with us, his faithful, on this condition, that if he does anything against the pact which unites us, we will admonish him with reverence to amend his conduct and maintain each of us in his rank and in his rights. And if he should refuse, be it known that we are all so united among ourselves, with the king's own knowledge and assent, that none of us will abandon his peer in such a way that the king is able to do anything against the law and against reason.'[21]

It is obvious that principles such as these were a severe check on the monarchy; and as long as they held firm, a restoration of royal power was out of the question. But the conditions they reflected were less the outcome than the cause of feudal reorganization; and it would be a mis-understanding to attribute to feudalism the anarchy of ninth- and tenth-century France. It was not feudalism that produced the collapse of the state, nor was it the cause of the transference into the hands of the princes of powers formerly exercised by the king. Feudalism is still often condemned as anarchical in tendency, a dissolvent of society. In fact, during the two centuries after 850, it was first and foremost an element of resistance to the total collapse of the social and political order,[22] not very effective at first, but more and more effective from the close of the tenth century.

For this reason feudalism has been described not as a source of anarchy, but as a reaction against anarchy.[23] For the old principles of government, which had perished, it substituted a new principle: the subordination of man to man, in a long hierarchy, through vassalage; a society based not on equality of all under the state and a direct connection between each individual and the government, but on classes and class-gradations, a hierarchical society. Politically this remained the basis of French society down to the middle of the thirteenth century. Socially, by way of the spread of French civilization through the crusades, the *Reconquista* in Spain, the Norman conquest of England, and later through the expansion of feudal ideas and attitudes to Germany in the twelfth century and to Bohemia, Poland and Hungary in the thirteenth and fourteenth centuries, it set the standard of European society for centuries to come, in some cases down to 1789 and beyond. That is why the origins and early development of French feudalism deserve more than passing attention. Rooted in France, it became, by expansion, from the end of the eleventh century onwards, a European feudalism.

Six Italian society from Charlemagne to Otto I

WHEN WE TURN from France to Italy, we find a very different line of development; and if we seek the basic reason for this difference, we shall find it in the fact that Frankish institutions, particularly the county, were not indigenous in Italy but superimposed at a relatively late date – in fact, after 774, too late to take root. Consequently, the county did not play the same fundamental part in Italian development as it did in France. The Frankish counts, imported into Italy by Charles the Great to serve Frankish interests, were simply put in the place of their Lombard predecessors; and the pre-Frankish Lombard administrative divisions, although henceforward in Frankish hands, remained as the basis of government.

Since the history of the Lombard monarchy and its administrative arrangements was very different from that of the Frankish monarchy, the outcome was also very different. The Lombard settlement of Italy was a settlement of military bands, under their leaders or 'dukes', who simply appropriated the Romano-Gothic cities and the surrounding territory; and the monarchy only gradually and imperfectly made headway against the dukes. Even when the monarchy began to make progress in internal consolidation – which was not until the first half of the eighth century under Liutprand (712–44) – it was substantially only in the Lombard plain that it secured effective predominance. Here it was able to control local government through its reeves, the *gastaldi*, in much the same way as the Frankish kings asserted control in Gaul through the counts; but the outlying duchies were a tougher problem, which remained unsolved by the time of the Frankish conquest.

The Franks, after 774, sought to consolidate their conquest by putting their own counts in place of the Lombard dukes and *gastaldi*; but the administration was not unified, and the fundamental difference between the smaller districts, the *gastaldati*, governed by the *gastaldi* on behalf of the Lombard king, and the greater duchies was not obliterated. This differentiation, as compared with the uniform county organization of Gaul, is the first distinguishing feature in Italian history in the late-Carolingian period. The second is the continuing importance of the cities, which had persisted through Lombard times. The third is the weakness, or backwardness, as compared with France, of feudalism; for feudalism in the Carolingian period was essentially a Frankish institution; it only

98

developed in Italy later and never with the same consistency, as a result of the ninth century invasions, which there as everywhere else created a new need for protection.

THE RISE OF THE MARQUESSES

As long as the strong hand of the Frankish kings was available to maintain control, these differences were kept submerged. But the partitions of the Frankish lands, and then the impact of the invasions, immediately brought them to the surface, and they became the decisive factors in Italian development. Above all else, the far-reaching differences between the core of the Lombard kingdom, the plain of Lombardy, which had been subject to the Lombard king, and the outlying provinces, became decisive. In Lombardy, much as in France, there was a series of small counts, successors of the *gastaldi* and all more or less equal; and among them none stood out as a natural leader. But, as foreigners, they were not so firmly seated as were their fellows in the west Frankish lands, and as the invasions disorganized government and stimulated the development of feudal relations, it was not round them that the new society crystallized, as it was doing at the same period in France. Far from playing into their hands, the dislocation of Carolingian government weakened their position, which had never ceased to be dependent upon the support and backing of the monarchy, and made it easy to displace them.

Outside Lombardy, however, the position was different. In Spoleto, for example, there was a Frankish family, which was successor to the great semi-independent Lombard dukes of Spoleto, and in the confusion and anarchy of civil war, this family, and others like it, quickly asserted its position of predominance over the smaller counts of the area, and rose to prominence. The result was that, in those parts of Italy – Spoleto, Tuscany and Friuli – which had stood outside the immediate sphere of action of the Lombard king and had never known the levelling effects of royal government, a process which in France took generations to complete – namely, the rise of the great territorial princes – was effected in a few years. The rise of the great Italian dynasties occurred almost entirely in the period 834–88; and when in 888, on the death of the Emperor Charles the Fat, the Carolingian empire finally disintegrated, there were three families ready to take the crown. All were foreigners, non-Italians;[1] all had started as Carolingian officials; but all used the advantages inherent in their position to draw ahead of their fellows, to subject the other counts to their authority, build a principality, and grasp after the Italian throne.

First in the field were the margraves or marquesses of Spoleto, Salian Franks who lost their French fiefs in 834 as supporters of Lothar, and withdrew with him to Italy. Their rise was stupendous: Guido or Guy of Spoleto was king of Italy in 889, emperor in 891; his son Lambert followed him from 891 to 898. They were eclipsed, however, by a second family, that of the dukes or marquesses of Friuli, from whom descended the king and emperor, Berengar I (898–924). This again was a Frankish family, which only received Friuli about 830; but succeeding to the

Lombard duke who had guarded the eastern confines of Lombardy, it quickly rose into the front rank.

Thirdly, there was the house of Tuscany, descendants of a Bavarian, Boniface count of Lucca. Their position was different from that of the other two, in so far as Tuscany was a later creation, similar to Flanders, established in the ninth century to defend the western seaboard of the peninsula against the Saracens.[2] But this special position enabled the counts of Lucca to rise into the front rank.

The political history of Italy after 888 is really the history of the struggles of these three great houses for hegemony and ultimately for the Italian crown. It was complicated by outside intervention from Provence and Burgundy, and by a growing tendency for intervention from Germany, culminating in Otto I's first Italian expedition in 951. As a result Hugh of Provence acquired the Italian throne in 926. It was also complicated by the rise of a fourth great house, that of Ivrea, descended from a certain Ansgario, a Frankish count from the region of Dijon, whom Guy of Spoleto had brought in – with many other Burgundians – at the very close of the ninth century, to take over the defence of the north-eastern frontier. Here again the exceptional powers granted for frontier defence enabled the new dynasty to rise at phenomenal speed, and in 950 it provided a king in the person of Berengar II. But above all, the position was complicated by the fact that none of these families was strong enough to dominate the others by its own efforts. Each and all, if they wished to gain and maintain their predominance, had to secure control of Lombardy itself. Thus the struggle may be summed up as a struggle for control of the Lombard plain; for without Lombardy none of the outlying pro-vinces, in the east or the west or south towards Rome, could hope to dominate the land.

The most obvious expedient to this end was to place their own sup-porters in the controlling positions as counts; and this policy was pursued by Guy of Spoleto, who imported large numbers of Burgundians, by Berengar of Friuli, and above all by Hugh of Provence, who brought his Provençal vassals with him and placed them in all the leading positions. 'It was impossible', says the Italian chronicler of the period, Liutprand of Cremona, 'to find an Italian who had not been either driven out or deprived of all his dignities.'

Fundamentally, this process was very important. It meant the dis-placement throughout Lombard Italy of the Carolingian aristocracy, and the importation of a new aristocracy from Burgundy and Provence, and thus an almost complete breach with the Carolingian past – a marked contrast with France, where the later feudal nobility descended directly from the Frankish counts. On the other hand, this rapid shift of personnel, together with the fact that the new counts were strangers and foreigners, weakened the position of the counts as a class, particularly in regard to the cities which they governed. In Italy, therefore, the late-Carolingian period saw not merely a thoroughgoing change in the personnel of the counts, but an even more important change in the position and importance of the county. Whereas in France the county was becoming the basis of the principality, in Italy it lost importance. The counts declined in status, their functions were limited, and many of their powers passed from them into the hands of the cities and particularly of the bishops, as representatives of the cities.

CITIES AND BISHOPS

In Italy the result of the Carolingian breakdown was, therefore, the decline of the county and the rise of the city. The reasons for this were many. In the first place, the city had always been more important in Italy than in Gaul, and it was not easy in any circumstances to subject it to the count's authority. Secondly, the effect of the invasions in Italy – that is, of the Magyar and Saracen invasions – was to throw the cities into prominence as centres of resistance. The counts were not strongly enough seated to lead the defence: in face of the invasions they appear to have capitulated, and the cities and the bishops, as the leading authorities in the cities, abandoned to their own devices, gained strength in looking after their own defence.

Moreover, the different kings after 888, in their endeavours to gain control of Lombardy, required support and were prepared to buy support by the grant of privileges to the bishops and the cities. This attempt to buy support was particularly marked under Berengar I at the beginning of the tenth century. The bulk of episcopal privileges in Italy date from the period between 904 and 922, and their effect was to introduce radical changes in the organization of Italian government. It is true that similar privileges were granted at the same period by the French and German rulers; but because there the cities were exceptional and counted little by comparison with the countryside, they did not affect the general picture. In Italy, where the city still remained the centre of government, it was otherwise. Guy and Lambert, Berengar and Rudolf, all the rulers from 888 to 926, granted the bishops charters permitting them to dig ditches, construct towers, build ramparts, maintain fortifications. But that was only a start. Because the bishop reconstructed and maintained the city fortifications, because this could not be done successfully without money and other resources, it was necessary for him also to exercise wider authority over the inhabitants. Thus, with the right of fortification went also other rights and privileges – rights of market, for example, and rights to tolls and public revenues – and finally exemption from the counts' jurisdiction. Step by step, in short, the count was excluded from the city: all powers necessary to organize defence, including in the end judicial power, were concentrated in the bishop's hands.[3]

This change, which was completed by the time Hugh of Provence arrived upon the scene in 926, was decisive both for the immediate political situation and in its long-term results. As far as the long-term results are concerned, it was the first stage in the process which was to make Italy a land of city-states. It was, of course, only the first stage. For one thing, the cities had only gained their independence from the county; they did not yet predominate over the counties and control the surrounding countryside, and this stage would not be reached until economic revival began in the eleventh century. In the second place, the cities had not yet attained self-government. At this stage the bishop was firmly entrenched as the representative of the city; in some cases he may have ruled in co-operation with an assembly of citizens, but the city government was still his government. Nor is there any sign of hostility or resistance on the part of the inhabitants to this state of affairs. They still willingly accepted episcopal leadership; and conflict between the citizens and the bishop arose only at a later period in Italian history. The charter of 904 for Bergamo, for example, was granted to the bishop and the *concives* jointly; this shows how the bishop and the body of citizens together sought and obtained privileges which made the city independent of the count and of the county.

The new powers acquired by the cities and the bishops between 888 and 926 are important because they fundamentally altered the position of the count in Italy. When Hugh of Provence brought in new men wholesale after 926, the autonomy of the cities had already been achieved, and the new counts simply ruled over the countryside outside the city walls. In the city the bishop had a position equivalent to that of the count. This was the situation throughout Lombardy; but it was not so further south in Tuscany and Spoleto, where the marquesses were strong enough to keep the cities in subjection. That is why, later, it was in Lombardy that the communal movement started, and only slowly penetrated from there into Tuscany and south to Rome. The result in Lombardy was, however, of great importance. It was not merely a pointer to the future rise of the Lombard communes but it also resulted in a fundamental breach with the past – that is to say, it brought about a form of political organization essentially different from that of Carolingian times, when the count had resided in the city and governed the countryside from the city.

From the beginning of the tenth century the count's power was confined to the countryside, and this was a major restriction on his authority, implying a sharp decline in his power and position. When economic recovery began, the economic strength of the towns meant that the countryside could not stand out against the city; and so one by one the counties would be mopped up and brought within the cities' sphere of interests and under their control. The next phase, therefore, would be the expansion of the cities at the expense of the counties, the process which Italian historians describe as the conquest of the *contado* by the commune.

If such, very briefly, were the long-term results of the impact of the Magyar and Saracen invasions on Italy, the immediate result was to place ultimate power in the hands of the Lombard bishops. They could not, perhaps, make a king; but no king could maintain his position for long without their support or against their opposition. The rivalry of the three or four great aristocratic families, none of which could prevail without their support, gave them their chance. Thus it was the bishops, led by the archbishop of Milan, who called in the duke of Burgundy against Berengar I in 923; it was the defection of the bishops which led to the fall of Hugh of Provence in 945; and finally it was the episcopal opposition which summoned Otto I to Italy in 951.

The marked tendency of the episcopate to look outside Italy for salvation may, at first sight, seem strange. But we have to remember, first, that none of the Italian dukes or marquesses was Italian in blood or descent, and that there was no question of an Italian kingship. More important, the instability of the duchies was a serious drawback for the church; none had in itself the resources to rule or to ward off invasion, all were opposed to the constitution of any power superior to themselves, and it seemed (and was probably true) that only a power with outside resources could restore the stability which the bishops needed to consolidate the gains they had made between 904 and 922. The position of the Italian kings between 888 and 962 – all upstarts, Carolingian nobles who had risen above their fellows – was inevitably precarious. To gain support they had to alienate lands, and none after a few years had adequate estates. If they wished to recover estates so as to establish a firmer government, they ran into episcopal opposition; if they placated the bishops, they had to resign all idea of recovering lost lands and rights.

These are the facts which explain the extraordinary instability of Italian history in this period, the constant revolutions, the rapid transference of power from one dynasty to another. It was only when Otto I intervened in 951 and then again ten years later, that – through the use of his German resources – stability, or at least relative stability, was restored. Because he had the resources of Germany behind him, he succeeded where earlier contenders for the Italian throne had failed. Even so, Otto I did not create a new order in Italy: he only stabilized and confirmed the changes which had taken place since 888. His rule was based throughout on the bishops, who originally had been instrumental in calling him in; and though he brought in German counts, particularly to control the northern passes connecting Germany and Italy, he accepted the changes in the position of the count, the decline which had occurred in the previous generation.

ITALY UNDER GERMAN RULE

Nevertheless, the establishment of German rule in 961–62 was in many respects a turning-point in Italian history. It brought to an end the conditions of anarchy which had prevailed for a century past; and this was a fact of cardinal importance. It meant that, by comparison with France, where, as we have seen, the princes only started the work of reconstruction in the eleventh century, recovery came more quickly in Italy. The stability restored by Otto was a precondition for the revival of commerce and the upsurge of agriculture in the eleventh century, which made the rise of the communes possible.

It is true that German government in Italy in the tenth and eleventh centuries was intermittent and often weak. It depended always on the co-operation of an Italian party, headed by the bishops, which had to be recompensed for its support of the German king. But it was better than the anarchy which had preceded it. Moreover, the new element of stability, the ability of the king to maintain some sort of order among the nobility, made possible a revival of the papacy, which had been all but submerged in the anarchy of the early tenth century. It was a slow revival with many setbacks, since German intervention in Rome was not continuous enough to prevent the papacy from falling back time and again under the domination of local Roman aristocratic families. It did not have permanent effects until the middle of the eleventh century when the emperor Henry III decided to make a clean sweep and replace the Italian popes by popes from north of the Alps, thus bringing a breath of fresh air into the Augean stables.

Nevertheless, it was not least among the results of the establishment of German rule by Otto I. After 888 the papacy, which a few years earlier, under Nicholas I, had seemed to be at the height of its power, an arbiter between the contending claimants to the imperial throne, was dragged down into Italian politics, and was on the point of losing any universal character it possessed, of becoming merely the puppet of Roman factions who placed their nominees on the papal throne simply as a move in the game of power-politics. The popes of this period are often described – with good reason – as profligate; but the fact, of course, is that they were noblemen, appointed for reasons of family policy or politics. The result, nevertheless, was that the papacy was on its way to losing both its moral prestige and its hold over Christendom, and becoming simply a small Italian territorial power.

Here again, therefore, Otto I's intervention, which inaugurated the process by which this period of decadence was ended, was crucial. The early death of his son, Otto II, the long minority that followed and the early death of Otto III, caused a setback; in the earlier part of the eleventh century the papacy again fell for a spell under the control of the counts of Tusculum. But here, as elsewhere in Italian affairs, the establishment of German government by Otto I marked the turning of the tide. German rule was too intermittent to produce anything like a 'new order', social or political; Otto I was content to regulate and stabilize and in that way to maintain control.[4] But by comparison with the preceding anarchy, the progress was real. On the other hand, the very stabilization and the economic recovery which ensued, brought new forces into play, which later were to turn against and destroy the Ottonian settlement. Meanwhile, what Italy needed was relief from the anarchy of the contending marquesses; and this Otto I gave it.

Seven

The rise of the German monarchy

THE REASON why Otto I was able to intervene in Italy in 951 was that, of all the lands which had been part of the Frankish dominions, Germany was the first to recover from late- and post-Carolingian anarchy. The explanation of this lies probably in part in the fact that, by comparison with France, Germany as a whole suffered less intensively and for a shorter period from the disorganizing effects of the invasions; but it was also due to characteristic differences in the history and political and social structure of the eastern and western halves of the Frankish kingdom.

It would, of course, be misleading, in this respect as in others, to speak of the east Frankish lands as a whole. The further west one went, in Franconia and the Rhinelands, the more conditions approximated to those of France. Furthermore, Bavaria, although it had maintained its political identity until late in the eighth century, had come under Frankish influence at an early date, and Frankish institutions, particularly vassalage and other elements of feudalism, had begun to percolate there also. Nevertheless, taking Germany as a whole, it is safe to say that feudalism had made nothing like the same headway as in the west Frankish lands in Carolingian times; Saxony in particular, even after the Frankish conquest, and the neighbouring region of Thuringia were essentially a land of peasants. The core of the army in the east was still composed largely of the contingents of peasant freemen; the heavily armed knight was an exceptional figure. And the aristocracy itself still clung to its freedom, for the most part rejecting vassalage and feudal ties as a sign of subjection and inferiority.

A second distinguishing factor in Germany was the persistence of a marked tribal differentiation. In the west the population had been fused together – not, indeed, to the degree of a complete destruction of racial and linguistic and cultural differences – by centuries of Frankish rule. In the east that was not so. The inclusion of Saxony and even of Bavaria in the Frankish realm was too recent to destroy entirely the older sense of separate national identity; and the different peoples, or 'stems', had their own distinctive legal codes. The effects are visible particularly in the military sphere. In the west Frankish kingdom, before the disappearance of the obligation on all free men to military service, the Carolingians directed their summons to the army to 'all inhabitants between Seine

39 Symbolic coronation of a German king by two archbishops

and Loire'. In Germany, on the other hand, the contingents were summoned people by people, race by race; in 869, for example, we find Louis the German dividing his army, sending Saxons and Thuringians to fight the Sorbs, the Bavarians against Moravia, and retaining the Franks and Swabians under his own command.

The third differentiating factor in Germany was the character of its organization in Carolingian times. Both for the defence of the eastern marches, and also to hold down the newly conquered provinces, extensive powers, far in excess of those of the west Frankish counts, were granted to the king's representatives. Because it was so largely exposed frontier land, the political organization of Carolingian Germany was very different from that of Carolingian France; practically speaking it was only in the old province of Franconia and in Lorraine – which, as we have seen, was only added to the eastern kingdom during the wars and partitions of late-Carolingian times – that anything like the Frankish county system of the west was in existence.

Fourth, and finally, it is fair to say that loyalty to the Carolingian dynasty and support for Carolingian policy were stronger in the east than in the west. This was no doubt due to the fact that the Frankish aristocracy in the east was not yet well rooted and had not had time to develop its own particular interests; that it still required, in a frontier area, the backbone of royal support. At any rate, it is noteworthy that it was in the west, not in the east, that aristocratic opposition, in which great prelates and nobles combined, first came to a head;[1] in the east, both church and nobility remained true far longer to Carolingian traditions, and it was only at a comparatively late date, when the east Frankish Carolingian dynasty died out, that serious political problems arose. In 888, there was no difficulty in electing the illegitimate Carolingian, Arnulf; nor on his death in 899, was there any difficulty about the succession of his son, Louis, although he was a mere child. And even on Louis the Child's death without heirs in 911, monarchical tradition – that is to say, the tradition of the Frankish monarchy – was still so strong that the transition to a new dynasty was carried through extraordinarily smoothly.

It is true that, roughly from 880 onwards, when the partition of the Carolingian lands had become final and irrevocable, a new spirit was arising in the east. The aristocracy, precisely because it was no longer a Frankish aristocracy with connections and properties in all parts of the Frankish dominions, began to concentrate more on its local interests; indeed, new non-Frankish families, who had risen in the service of the later east Frankish kings, came to the fore.[2] Frankish influence was weaker, Frankish predominance less sure. But right down to the end of the ninth century aristocracy and bishops remained loyal supporters of the king; they did not pursue independent territorial interests against the crown; and it was still the king, not the nobility, who determined policy. In all this there is a very marked contrast with the west, and still more with Italy, where the leading aristocratic families were striving after the crown. In Germany, in short, there was no total breakdown.

Difficulties began substantially in the first decade of the tenth century, when the weak and ineffective rule of Louis the Child coincided with the most severe phase of Magyar and Viking invasion. Only six years old when he succeeded in 900, Louis was perforce nothing more than a nominal king, and actual government, above all the task of defence against the Magyars, necessarily passed into the hands of the aristocracy. Franconia was rent by internal aristocratic feuds, and the rest of the land was desolated by Hungarian raids, against which the royal government was helpless. The result was the growth of local self-help, the same over-riding need for defence as in France.

But because conditions in east and west were not the same, the reaction to the invasions was different. The slower development of feudalism in the eastern lands prevented the fractioning of public powers in the hands of the feudatories; the existence of great military commanders along the frontiers, with powers far in excess of those of the counts, made these commanders the natural leaders of resistance. Whereas in France at the beginning of the tenth century some thirty distinct territorial divisions can be traced, and the land was torn by the rivalry of a multitude of equal contending powers, Carolingian counts and their successors, the east Frankish or German kingdom at the same period was composed of five (or, including Lorraine, of six) great duchies: namely, Franconia, Swabia, Thuringia, Saxony and Bavaria. Of these the small duchy of Thuringia was merged with Saxony, and disappeared from the scene after 908.[3] Lorraine, with a distinctive position from the start, threw in its lot with the west in 911, and was only brought back under German rule in 925.

If Lorraine, which was simply the remnant of the artificially created 'middle kingdom' of Lothar, is left out of account, it is evident that all these duchies were the successors of the independent pre-Frankish German tribes; and their appearance at the end of the ninth century has consequently been described as a 'resurrection of the ancient Germanic nations', which, 'owing to the stress of the time', instinctively and spontaneously rallied 'around their natural and historical tribal representatives'.[4] But this traditional view is difficult to reconcile with the facts. If we examine the history of the families which rose to prominence at the end of the ninth and the beginning of the tenth centuries, between 888 and 918, it is evident that they were not 'natural and historical tribal representatives', but people who used the special powers and position given them in the Carolingian scheme of government to extend their authority, in time of need, over the counts of their area, and then over the inhabitants. In Swabia, Bavaria, Thuringia and Saxony, the dukes of early tenth-century Germany were the successors of the frontier commanders; only in the west, in Franconia and Lorraine, was the position different, for here no authority was set above the counts, and here therefore, as in France, there was a struggle of all against all, until one comital family obliterated and prevailed over its rivals.

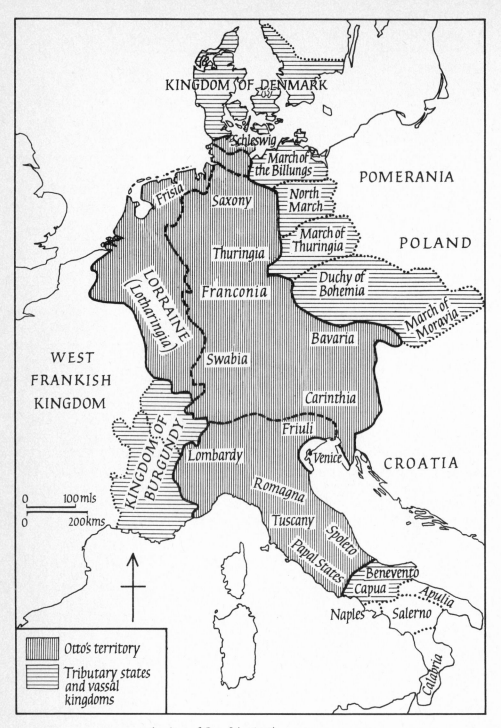

KINGDOM OF DENMARK

Schleswig

March of
the Billungs

POMERANIA

Frisia

Saxony

North
March

POLAND

Thuringia

March of
Thuringia

Franconia

Duchy of
Bohemia

March of
Moravia

LORRAINE
(Lotharingia)

Bavaria

WEST
FRANKISH
KINGDOM

Swabia

Carinthia

Friuli

Venice

CROATIA

KINGDOM OF
BURGUNDY

Lombardy

Romagna

0   100 mls

0   200 kms

Tuscany

Spoleto

Papal States

Benevento

Capua

Apulia

Naples

Salerno

Calabria

Otto's territory

Tributary states
and vassal
kingdoms

40 Europe at the time of Otto I (936–73)

In Franconia the struggle between the two rival dynasties, the 'Conradiner' and the Babenbergs, lasted a generation, and was only decided in 906 by the murder of the last of the Babenbergs, which left their rivals in control; for no other family in Franconia could equal the Conradiner in wealth and power. Elsewhere the process was more straightforward. The dukes of Saxony, later kings of Germany, sprang from a certain count Liudolf, described about 860 as *dux orientalis Saxoniae*, i.e. military commander (the original sense of the word *dux*) on the eastern frontiers of Saxony. In Thuringia, in the same way, power devolved into the hands of counts who had the title *duces Sorabici limitis*, i.e. commanders of the frontier against the Slav tribe of Sorbs; though, as already noted, their independent position did not last beyond 908. In Bavaria the ducal family of the early tenth century descended from a certain Liutpold, who fell in 907 as leader of the Bavarian levy in battle against the Hungarians; he was entitled in a royal charter of 903 *dux Boemanorum*, and that means not duke of Bavaria, but military commander on the frontiers of Bohemia. And though in Swabia there were more competitors for the leading place, and a struggle ensued not unlike that in Franconia, control eventually came into the hands of a man whose title is *dux Raetiarum*, i.e. defender of the Swiss or Rhaetian frontier.

It is not difficult to see how military leaders of this type might use their military power to extend their authority. So as to secure additional forces against the invaders, to build up their powers of resistance, the 'dukes' took responsibility for the defence of their peoples, whom the weak monarchy was unable to protect, and gradually, in virtue of their power and wealth and authority, made themselves the representatives of the peoples of their areas. This was the position at the beginning of the tenth century, in the time of Louis the Child.[5] It was only a beginning. The position of none was secure. Even the title of 'duke' was not yet fixed. But the course of events, above all the pressure of invasion, had thrown up in each region leaders of power and authority, who because of their leadership and services in defence could invoke the loyalty and support of the inhabitants. There is no sign at this stage on their part of hostility to the monarchy, of a striving for independence or of the pursuit of an independent policy. The loyalty of the dynasty of Liudolf in Saxony to the east Frankish Carolingians is proverbial. Nevertheless, they were a power in the state, and a new power which had arisen since the partition of 887–88.

This was the position in 911 on the death of Louis the Child. His death raised the question of succession in a form without parallel in the past, since with Louis the line of east Frankish Carolingians became extinct. Traditionally, the designation of a new king was a matter for the royal dynasty; but with the extinction of the dynasty the traditional course was not possible. One alternative would have been to revert to the remaining Carolingian line, to Charles the Simple of France; and that, in fact, was what the Lotharingians did. But the west Frankish Carolingian, who had his hands full dealing with the Normans, could not be expected to provide help and leadership to the Germans in the east; and help and leadership against the Magyars was the first necessity. Hence in 911 the question arose of choosing a non-Carolingian king; and in view of the prominence possessed by the dukes by this time, it is not surprising that the decision devolved on them. What is surprising is the speed, the unanimity and the fidelity to Frankish tradition with which they made their decision.

No doubt the external dangers helped to create unity; but the dangers in the west were as great, and there unity was conspicuous by its absence. The difference in the east lay deeper; namely, in the fact that the east Frankish leaders were not feudal princes, intent on their own feudal interests, but still regarded themselves first and foremost as pillars of the monarchy, committed to the maintenance of royal interests. Hence they agreed without difficulty to make Conrad of Franconia king. The reason is obvious. It was not that he was the strongest of the dukes – he was not – but that, the Carolingian line having perished, he was, as duke of Franconia, the representative of the Frankish people in Germany. Thus, the leaders chose as successor the nearest possible person to the preceding king, and maintained the Frankish character of the monarchy. Nothing shows better how strong, compared with the west and with Italy, the Carolingian tradition was.

Yet Conrad I's reign (911–18) was a watershed. His position was obviously different from that of his predecessors on the east Frankish throne. He was, to be sure, a Frank, but he was not a Carolingian; indeed, he was simply the strongest of the Franconian counts who, after bloody and bitter struggles with the rival comital family of Babenberg, had wiped out his rivals. If in 911 he was made king, it still remained a fact that he was raised to the throne by men who were his equals in wealth and status. To have recognized these facts, to have ruled in harmony with the other great leaders, would have been wise policy. Unfortunately, Conrad did nothing of the sort. On the contrary, he was determined to rule as a Carolingian, and indeed as one of the great Carolings. Far from ruling in harmony with the other magnates of the realm, his aim was to bring under his authority the very persons who had given him that authority. He quarrelled with Henry of Saxony, trying to weaken the latter by depriving him of a part of his lands; he quarrelled similarly with Erchanger of Swabia and Arnulf of Bavaria. Above all else he tried to play off the church against the lay nobility; persuading the prelates at the famous Synod of Hohenaltheim (916) to impose the ban of the church on all, whatever their rank or dignity, who opposed the prerogatives of the king.

Meanwhile the Hungarians remained unchecked; instead of turning his royal power against the external foe, Conrad – who had been made king primarily to provide leadership against the invaders – used his power against the magnates, or else in unavailing efforts to bring Lorraine back under German control. And none of his efforts succeeded. Against Saxony he was forced simply to give up the struggle; and in the last years of the reign, duke Henry ruled there to all intents in independence, even the bishops (with one exception) remaining under his control. This unsuccessful policy inevitably provoked a hostile reaction. The king and the aristocratic leaders, who had worked together until 911, were alienated; the dukes were forced by Conrad into political opposition.

Hence the years of Conrad's reign are decisive. The dukes now set about organizing their position in opposition to the king. Down to 911 they had been satisfied to wield their powers under the king; after 911 that was no longer the case. By 918 they were for all practical purposes as powerful in their duchies as, a generation or two earlier, petty kings such as Boso of Vienne, Rudolf of Burgundy or Zwentibold of Lorraine had been in their *regna*. First, they set out to secure hereditary succession, and at the same time to obtain the assent and allegiance of the population of their duchy. Secondly, they began to claim and exercise control over the churches of their land – hitherto a distinctively royal prerogative – nominating to bishoprics and abbeys and sharing in clerical income. Thirdly, they brought the counts into dependence upon themselves, so far as they were able. And fourthly – and perhaps most characteristic of all – we find them pursuing an independent foreign policy, particularly the duke of Swabia in relation to the neighbouring kingdom of Burgundy and the duke of Bavaria in relation to Lombardy. The powers they assumed were, evidently, regal or semi-regal in character; they were powers not under, but against, the crown.

THE KING AGAINST THE DUKES

Thus the German duchy, as an institution, was the creation of the period 911–18. At the time of Conrad I's death in 918, the dukes were a new and powerful factor in the political situation; and it was a moot question whether the east Frankish lands would break up into a number of principalities or kingdoms, in the same way as the west Frankish kingdom had done, or whether the position of the monarchy, weakened though it was by Conrad, would survive. In fact, the monarchy survived. In part, that result was due to Conrad himself, whose one statesmanlike act was to perceive on his deathbed his own failure, and to designate as his successor the powerful duke of Saxony, Henry I. This act showed a recognition of the need for an effective monarchy which contrasts markedly with the attitude in the west Frankish kingdom at the same date. The reason is the maintenance in the east, down at least to the death of Arnulf in 899, of a strong royal tradition, far older than the newly arisen duchies. The authority of the dukes was 'a revolutionary power', born of opposition to Conrad; it was only the product of a few years, whereas the authority of the king reached back to the height of the Carolingian monarchy.

In actual fact, there was in 918 no question of a partition of the kingdom among the dukes. The need for a king was taken for granted by all parties, and the only question was to decide who was to take over in Conrad's place, who was to succeed to the Carolingian inheritance. In practice, the nomination of his successor by Conrad I decided the issue. At a meeting of the Franks and Saxons, Conrad's brother, Eberhard, as the representative of the Frankish people, handed over the royal insignia to the Saxon duke; and thereafter the gathering gave its allegiance to the new king. There was therefore no question of a formal election; the decisive fact was the designation of his successor by the preceding ruler. The further question, of course, was whether this act – the act of the Franks and Saxons alone – would be accepted by the other peoples; and this was the critical point. In fact, both Swabia and Bavaria opposed Henry's succession – a sign of how far provincial differences had proceeded since 911. The opposition of Swabia was soon overcome, though not without a military campaign; that of Bavaria lasted longer, and duke Arnulf of Bavaria was actually set up in opposition to Henry as 'anti-king'. Finally, in 921, he accepted Henry's position as ruler, but his assent had to be bought by major concessions, notably control over the bishoprics and royal abbeys in Bavaria, and he continued to pursue an independent policy.

Nevertheless the unity of the east Frankish kingdom was maintained, and this was the immediately important consideration. Moreover, the wealthy Saxon house, which now took over for a century, brought to the monarchy substantial landed property, and so there was never the risk of the kingship becoming, through lack of resources, a mere title as it was in the case of the later Carolingians in France. Though Conrad I's reign had provoked reaction, the solid tradition of one king and one kingdom – the Carolingian tradition – prevailed. The persistence of the Carolingian tradition in Germany is, therefore, a decisive fact, differentiating the east from the west Frankish lands and from Italy. It is seen again in the Italian policy of Henry I and his son, Otto I – a continuation of late-Carolingian precedents – and in the German king's relations with the church. All in all it is fair to say that the maintenance of the royal prerogatives handed down from the Carolingians was the factor enabling the German rulers of the new Saxon dynasty to rise above the dukes and then to assert their pre-eminence in western Europe.

Nevertheless, Henry I's position in 919 was far from secure, and it was evident that, if he were to do better than Conrad, he must avoid Conrad's mistakes, and above all not attack the dukes head-on, as Conrad had done. Any attempt to set the clock back, to destroy the duchies, was bound to provoke the same opposition that Conrad had incurred; and there is in fact no indication whatever that Henry had such ideas. He was a duke himself had ruled as one of them. His aim was not to destroy the duchies which had arisen in the previous twenty years, but rather to give them a fixed place in the system of government, subordinate to the monarchy, and thus to bring them under control. The powers asserted by the dukes were not yet firmly anchored in the constitution; they could still be moulded and reduced to reasonable proportions. This was the line Henry followed. And in this task, proceeding slowly and cautiously, and intervening only where he had every prospect of success, Henry I was

41 Henry the Wrangler, duke of Bavaria, who led an unsuccessful uprising against
Otto II

gradually successful. His success was due, in part at least, to the fact that, unlike Conrad, he took the lead in resistance to the Magyars, building fortifications – like Alfred in England[6] – along the eastern frontier of Saxony. In this way royal leadership was reaffirmed, and the roots of ducal independence – which lay in defence against the invaders – were sapped. Similarly in the west, he exploited the anarchy and confusion in the west Frankish kingdom to win back Lorraine, another royal achievement which raised the monarchy above the dukes. Nevertheless, the speed of his success must not be exaggerated. The question of the duchies remained the main internal problem throughout Henry I's own reign (919–36) and that of his son Otto I (936–73), and was only really settled when Otto II defeated the great Bavarian rebellion of 975.

In its dealings with the dukes, the new dynasty proceeded piecemeal. Henry I concentrated on the reassertion of royal control in Swabia. Otto I continued in Bavaria what his father had succeeded in doing in the south-west. In both cases, the main issues were the same: to regain control over the royal demesnes within the duchy; to break the duke's control over the church in his land, reaffirm the direct connection between the crown and the church, and thus to make the church, as it had been in Carolingian times, a pillar and support of the monarchy; to restore royal control over the counts, instead of leaving them to become the duke's dependants; and in regard to the duke himself, to break the practice of hereditary succession, which was becoming usual in 919 at the time of Henry I's accession, to assert the king's right to nominate the duke, and so to make the duke responsible to the monarchy.

In Swabia this was achieved by 926, when a new duke, nominated by the king, was appointed – a duke who was not a Swabian but a Frank, and who had therefore no roots in the duchy. In Bavaria royal intervention came only at the beginning of Otto I's reign, when the new duke, Eberhard, who had succeeded his father in 935, refused to do homage. The king's reply was to depose him, to set aside also the other sons of duke Arnulf, and to confer the Bavarian duchy on their uncle, Berthold of Carinthia, who was forced to agree that he would appoint neither bishops nor counts. Success, in the case of Bavaria, was only temporary. Otto had to face a second major revolt between 953 and 955, and another, more formidable still, occurred at the beginning of Otto II's reign.

But the king's attitude is nevertheless noteworthy. He made no attempt to suppress the duchy – he probably perceived that some such intermediate authority was necessary in a country as large as Germany – but sought instead, by putting in men from outside, to weaken its roots in the land and to tie it to the monarchy. Only in the case of Franconia was his attitude different. Eberhard of Franconia, who, as the executor of his brother's wishes in 918, had designated Henry I as king, remained a loyal supporter of Henry I to the end of his reign; and it was probably the joint support of Franconia and Saxony that enabled Henry to hold his own against and prevail over Bavaria and Swabia. But in 939, at the beginning of Otto I's reign, Eberhard of Franconia rebelled. This time, after the rebellion had been put down, Otto acted differently. No successor was appointed. Instead Franconia, the specifically Frankish region of the east, where the major part of the old Carolingian royal demesnes was located, remained henceforth under direct royal control.

In Saxony also, in 919, the new dynasty had appointed no duke, retaining instead its own position at the head of the Saxon people, and also the material resources flowing from its own considerable Saxon estates. Thus with the resources of Saxony and Franconia behind it, the royal dynasty had – very different from the French kings of the period – the material strength to ensure its own preponderance, and to bring the remaining dukes into dependence, or else to replace them by members of the royal house. The second method, used more sparingly, was to weaken the duchies by territorial amputation. Thus Lorraine, placed for a time under Otto I's brother, archbishop Bruno of Cologne, was divided into two, and Bavaria lost its two marches, the Nordgau lying towards the Bohemian frontier, and the Ostmark, from which the duchy of Austria was later to spring.

Finally, the crown turned more and more to the church. This was essentially the policy of Otto I – for Henry I, with memories of Conrad's reign, had tended to keep the church at arm's length – and dates substantially from the time of the rebellion of 953–55, which seems to have driven home to Otto the fact that his position was still in need of strengthening. Consequently, after 955 he began to develop the church systematically as a pillar of the monarchy. Here again there was a major difference from France, where (as we have seen) a large proportion of the bishoprics and abbeys were 'mediatized' and passed under the control of the feudal princes. In Germany, on the other hand, royal control over the church was the rule from 938, and was pretty well unchallenged after 975. All bishoprics were 'royal'; and by 951 Otto I was strong enough to assert that all 'royal' abbeys – they numbered eighty-five by the end of the tenth century – were exempt from any secular authority save that of the crown, and forbidden to enfeoff their lands without the consent of the king. These episcopal and monastic lands were thus 'enclaves' within the duchies, through which the king could make his power felt; and by granting the bishops and monastic churches 'immunity' – that is, by taking them out of the ordinary local administration and constituting their estates into 'liberties' or 'franchises' – the sphere of control of the secular magnates was steadily diminished. The church thus became the favoured instrument of the crown, and indeed one of its main resources. Already by the end of the tenth century it provided the backbone of the army: 74 per cent, for example, of the forces for Otto II's Italian campaign of 981 were provided by German abbeys and bishoprics, only 26 per cent by lay magnates.

THE WORK OF OTTO I: AN APPRAISAL

If we stop at this point and take stock of the work of internal reorganization carried through by Henry I and Otto I in Germany between 919 and 973, we may be content with the judgment[7] that for the time being they had built well. The contrast in 973 with France, where the Carolingian dynasty was on the point of expiry, and with Italy, is remarkable. Only in the east had the Carolingian structure of government weathered the storm. Only in the east had a dissolution of the state been avoided, and the near-anarchy of contending powers – never in any case so serious as elsewhere – had lasted at longest from 899 to 919, less than a generation.

On the other hand, we must not exaggerate the degree of Ottonian success. If Otto I built well, it was only 'for the time'. There were definite limitations to what he achieved. First of all, even in the question of the duchies, to place them in the hands of members of his family was no permanent solution; rather it created the danger, which flared up in 953, of dynastic rivalries. Secondly, his use of the church produced quick results, because churchmen – frightened at the prospect of falling under the power of rapacious laymen – were prompt to grasp the opportunity of co-operating with the crown. But the result of royal reliance on the church was that the lay aristocracy, given little share in the work of government, tended more and more to withdraw into isolation and concentrate on building up its own estates. And though it is certainly true that no king in the tenth century could have foreseen the later demands for a church free from royal control, the fact remains that exclusive reliance on the church was dangerous, particularly as the higher ranks of the clergy were still essentially aristocratic. Bishops and abbots were regularly selected from the great noble families, and there was no guarantee that they would continue for all time to side with the monarchy against the aristocracy. And finally, the very success of the king in his dealings with the dukes created new problems, for in a country the size of Germany intermediate authorities to help the crown in the task of government were needed, and it was precisely these authorities that Otto I had weakened. Thus it is possible to say of Ottonian government in Germany that, in reviving Carolingian traditions of government, it was archaic and backward-looking, a retarding influence, which introduced no new initiative, but simply drew upon the past for its strength and with the passage of time became more and more out of date.[8]

However, these limitations, which were to be a serious source of weakness in the future, were a source of strength in the present. Contrasted with the anarchy of France and Italy, Carolingian methods of government were effective, and gave the king a power possessed by no other ruler in the west. Hence the Ottonian dynasty was able to use the quick recovery of Germany from anarchy to build up for itself a position of preponderance in continental Europe. In regard to the west, it intervened in the contest between Carolingians and Capetians in such a way as to hold a balance between the parties and prevent any French attempt at the recovery of Lorraine. In the east, no sooner were the Hungarian incursions checked, than the German rulers went over from defence to attack, thrusting forward beyond the Elbe towards the river Oder. This first phase of the German *Drang nach Osten*, of eastward expansion, was not a success; it was brought to a halt and reversed by the great Slav uprising in 983, and was only resumed a century and a half later. It is nevertheless a significant indication of the strength and energy of the German monarchy that it was so quick, and so ruthless, in embarking in this way on war against the Slav peoples living beyond its eastern frontier.

And just as Henry and Otto intervened in east and west, so they intervened in the German interest in the south. Henry I's intervention was directed mainly against the kingdom of Burgundy, but there is reliable evidence that, at the time of his death in 936, he was planning an expedition to Italy. His son carried on where he had left off. On the death in 937 of Rudolf of Burgundy, he intervened as protector of Rudolf's heir; and though Burgundy remained independent for another century, ultimate German control was assured. In Italy he sought at first – in the same way as he did in France – to maintain a balance of power between Hugh of Provence and Berengar of Ivrea; but when the former died and the latter looked like gaining complete control, Otto intervened. That was in 951. The civil war of 953–55 in Germany prevented Otto from exploiting his success, and Berengar again built up his strength, striking south towards Rome. As a result of this threat pope John XII, who saw his temporal power in Rome in danger of disappearing, called on the German ruler for aid; and in 961 Otto again appeared in Italy, expelled Berengar, secured the Lombard crown at Pavia, and then proceeded south to Rome for imperial coronation. In 962 he was crowned emperor by the pope, and therewith became ruler of all the non-Byzantine lands of Italy.

Parallels have often been drawn between the coronation of 962 and that of 800. But the differences are greater than the similarities, not least of all because the events of the ninth century had destroyed the universal significance of the imperial title.[9] It has often been said that Otto saw himself as the heir or descendant of Charles the Great. But from the time of the emperor Lothar's death in 855, from the time of the emperor Louis II, the imperial title had been confined to Italy; and there is little to show that Otto regarded it as more than the rightful confirmation of his Italian victories. There was no attempt to extend his rule over all the Frankish lands, as they had been constituted under Charlemagne. Otto's power was confined to Germany and Italy only. Later, in 1034, Burgundy was annexed; but the new empire never implied more than rule over Germany, Italy and Burgundy.

It is true that Otto and his successors, as rulers of Italy, had a special relationship with the pope; and in course of time this result of the acquisition of the imperial title became an important factor in European history. Whether the connection with the papacy was important for Otto is less clear. It has been argued that, because of his great reliance in German government on the church, it was necessary for him to get control of the papacy, and that for this reason he sought the imperial title. But this view exaggerates the influence of the tenth-century papacy – which, as we have seen, was morally and in every other way at a low ebb – and at the same time underestimates the bonds of interest which bound the German church to the royal dynasty, to say nothing of the church's unquestioned acceptance of Otto's dominion as the divinely appointed governor of the church in his lands. The conquest of Italy, and with it, as a natural corollary, the acquisition of the imperial title, was in reality little more than a consequence of the fact that Germany, of all the lands of western Europe, had recovered first from the late-Carolingian anarchy, and was therefore in a position to make its power felt. To look for deeper motives – such as the leadership of Christendom against the heathen – as German historians have done, is more apt to confuse than to clarify. Nor, it should be added, is there any sign of the influence of Roman ideas, of a revival or 'renovatio' of the Roman empire, nor even – as in the case of Charles the Great – of equality with Byzantium. This may have been the case under Otto III; it was not so in 962.

For Otto I the basis of his empire was conquest. He came to Rome as a conqueror, and was treated and regarded there as a conqueror; the Roman people, led by the aristocracy, looked down on the 'raw Saxons', and did all they could to throw off the German yoke. No sooner was Otto's back turned than, in 963, led by the pope who had crowned him, the first revolt flared up. It was cruelly suppressed, as were succeeding revolts; the ringleaders were hanged or transported. If it is a commonplace that Charles the Great's seat of power remained north of the Alps even after he was crowned emperor in Rome, it is even more true that the basis of Otto's imperial power was German might, German troops, German arms. In north Italy, indeed, he ruled, as we have seen, by building up a party among the bishops, tied to him, like the German bishops, by privileges and common interests. Otherwise his empire was based on German power and there was a growing tendency to place loyal Germans in Italian bishoprics.

Nevertheless, this power was a reality, and it is also necessary to add that in the conditions of the time it was beneficial. Whatever else, it restored stability and order, and that, after the anarchy of the invasions, was the first necessity. And the further German conquests extended, the greater was the area stabilized. Italy itself ceased to be a land of contending dynasties. Burgundy, after its annexation in 1034, was at any rate more settled than previously, though here in fact the German ruler did less than elsewhere to intervene effectively. Lorraine also, torn by feudal strife during its brief period of independence, was more settled, though never effectively settled. The German kings, in fact, took on more than they could achieve; the very extent of their rule militated, in a period when communications were tenuous and difficult, against uniformly effective government. But that, all in all, it meant a restoration of a higher level of order in a major part of western Europe, is beyond doubt; and such a restoration of order was a condition of further progress. In this sense the establishment of the Ottonian empire in 962 may be taken as a turning-point in European history. France still stood apart, submerged in feudal disorder. England, still outside the main stream, followed a path of its own. But elsewhere, from 962, we are again, after the setbacks beginning under Louis the Pious, at the start of a new period of progress; and this benefit, which overrides much else, must be attributed in large measure to the Saxon dynasty.

42 Tenth-century ivory plaque of an emperor (Otto I?) presenting a church to Christ

43, 44 The religious and martial views of kingship: above, Otto II and Theophanu with the future Otto III at Christ's feet; right, the king with orb and sceptre, and his warriors below him

Eight   **The Anglo-Saxon achievement**

IF THE YEAR 962 marked the beginning of a new period in the lands ruled by Otto I, it also seemed by this date that Anglo-Saxon England had emerged from the trials and tribulations of the Danish wars, which began in 835 and continued almost without intermission for over a century. The reign of Edgar (959–75) was a time of external peace and internal stability, and there is no more striking evidence of the change of atmosphere and the return of more settled conditions than the revival of English monasticism and the reform of the English church inaugurated by Edgar's close associate, St Dunstan, who became archbishop of Canterbury in 960.

This recovery – though it was halted by a new wave of Danish invasions which began in 980, only five years after Edgar's death – was all the more remarkable when we consider that no country in western Europe was more severely tested by the Viking raids than England. Elsewhere, the Vikings plundered and devastated; in France they occupied and colonized the area along the lower reaches of the Seine which was later to be the duchy of Normandy; but in England alone was there a concerted effort to conquer the whole country and bring it under Danish rule. By 876 this assault had almost succeeded. Of the four Anglo-Saxon kingdoms which had existed in 840, only Wessex in the south and south-west maintained a precarious existence. East Anglia was occupied in 869 and 870; the Mercian ruler was driven out in 874 and his kingdom dismembered and divided; and in 876 the southern half of Northumbria, corresponding to the old kingdom of Deira and the modern county of York, was allotted to Danish colonists. In 877 it was the turn of Wessex. In a winter campaign the Danes overran most of the country. A large part of the West Saxon people submitted to Danish rule, and the West Saxon king was forced to withdraw to the safety of Athelney, an inaccessible island surrounded by marsh and swamp in a remote corner of Somerset.

On the surface, the outstanding feature of the next seventy years is the recovery of Wessex, beginning with Alfred's victory at Eddington in 878, and the gradual extension of the rule of the West Saxon kings over the remaining Anglo-Saxon regions, notably West Mercia, and over the lands occupied by the Danish conquerors.[1] This was essentially

45 King Edgar offering the charter of Winchester Minster to Christ; from a tenth-century document

the work of Alfred's successors, Edward the Elder (899–924) and Athelstan (924–39), and, considering the odds against them, it was by any standard a remarkable achievement. But no less significant, by comparison with the situation on the European mainland, were the measures by which it was accomplished. Instead of a dissolution of society and a total breakdown of government, as in the west Frankish lands, the effect of the Danish invasions in England was to provoke a vigorous reaction on the part of the monarchy, not dissimilar from but far more coherent and systematic than that of the two contemporary German rulers, Henry I and Otto I. Moreover, whereas the Saxon dynasty in Germany reverted to Carolingian tradition, modelling its government, as far as possible, on that of its Carolingian predecessors, with few, if any, significant innovations, the West Saxon kings in England created, almost from nothing, a new and remarkably efficient administrative organization, the essential features of which persisted through the period of Danish rule under Canute and his sons (1016–42) and the conquest of England by the Normans in 1066, and laid the foundations of English government for centuries to come.

The years between the death of Alfred in 899 and the death of Edgar in 975 were thus on all counts one of the decisive formative periods in English history. If we compare the position at the beginning of the ninth century before the beginning of the Danish invasions, and the position a century and a half later at the accession of Edgar, or still more at the time of the Norman conquest in 1066, it is evident that nothing less than a revolution in government had taken place. Somewhere in the century and a half before 1066 a complete network of hundreds and shires had been created, a network which (though with many changes of boundaries) constituted the framework of local government down to modern times. At the same time, by comparison with the earlier phases of Anglo-Saxon kingship, there was a rapid growth of royal power, marked by the merging of the ancient tribal divisions in a single kingdom. New ties were established between the monarchy and the people, as the king, with his own laws and procedures, laid the foundations of a royal legal system, which began to take the place of the old local laws. The contrast with the continent, where royal initiative was at a low ebb and law-making non-existent, could scarcely be more pronounced, and Heinrich Mitteis, better placed than most English historians to make such a comparison, was surely right when he concluded that the Anglo-Saxon monarchy in the tenth century was 'distinctly stronger' than any other in western Europe.[2]

THE REORGANIZATION OF LOCAL GOVERNMENT

To assess the achievement of the West Saxon monarchy after 899 it is necessary to put it in historical perspective. In the first place, we should not forget how small, by comparison with either the west Frankish or the east Frankish dominions, the kingdom of Wessex was. From this point of view, if we wish to make a comparison, it should be with one of

46, 47 The so-called 'Alfred Jewel' (ninth century), and a gold dinar of Offa of Mercia (late eighth century)

the German dukes or French princes, rather than with the later Carolingians or their successors in the east. Secondly, we must remember that Anglo-Saxon England had never, in the period before the Danish invasions, been one country under a single ruler, and there was therefore no question of defending or maintaining an existing unity. For one moment it had seemed that Offa of Mercia, the contemporary of Charles the Great, would bring the other Anglo-Saxon kingdoms under his rule; but even he failed to reduce Wessex to dependence, and after his death in 796 the ascendancy of Mercia quickly collapsed. On the whole, the history of Anglo-Saxon England until the ninth century was less like that of the Frankish lands north of the Alps, where some sort of unity had been imposed from the time of Clovis, than like that of Lombard Italy where, as we have seen,[3] the leaders of the warbands which had settled the land had resisted all efforts to unify the country under a single dynasty until the eve of its conquest by Charles the Great in 774.

In addition – no doubt in part because none of the royal dynasties was strong enough to establish a really dominating position for itself – Anglo-Saxon government at this period was extremely rudimentary, even by the standards of Merovingian Gaul. So far as the sparse and fragmentary records allow us a glimpse of it, what we see is an aristocratic society, in which the monarchy still played a very limited part.[4] The kings' main concern was the collection of their dues – principally the food-rents owed to them and their household servants as they travelled the land – and for this they relied upon the reeves who administered their estates or manors. Beyond this, administration was a burden, not a profit, and it is only necessary to read the early Anglo-Saxon laws, with their elaborate tariffs for every kind of offence, to see that the object was to avoid litigation, for which there was no adequate machinery. In the last resort, of course, the king himself or his reeves had to do justice; but every endeavour was made to ensure that recourse to the monarchy 127 would be the last resort. In short, the administration – if it is not an exaggeration at this stage to speak of an administration – was not founded, like so much later medieval administration, on law enforcement and the king's position as the guardian of justice; still less was it founded on the shouldering of public burdens. On the contrary, it was founded, to the exclusion almost of all else, on the exaction of rights and tributes and dues. It was the primitive administration of a predatory kingship, lording it over subjected peoples and conquered territories, and nowhere is there visible a popular element or popular courts.

The Danish invasions to all intents and purposes swept away this primitive social and political organization. As in the Frankish lands on the continent, war was a potent cause of innovation: it swept away a mass of debris and reduced life to the elemental satisfaction of basic needs. Not only did the kingdoms of northern England and the Midlands collapse, and with them such rudimentary political institutions as they had evolved. In addition, the devastation of war, and the deliberate destruction of supplies which might fall into the invaders' hands, dealt a deadly blow to agriculture. People were uprooted; land remained untilled. And with a large floating population of dispossessed or displaced persons, the bulk without regular means of subsistence, crime and lawlessness increased, from murder and rape to theft, particularly cattle-stealing. The thief, and more generally the lawbreaker, became for the first time in English history (so far as we know) a major social problem, demanding energetic action.

To begin with, however, the pressing need was military, and the necessary military measures were taken in hand by Alfred the Great (871–99). The history of Alfred's reign and his own character as a leader are entangled in propaganda and myth,[5] but it is obvious that his essential contribution was stubborn defence. His actual achievement was limited. When he died in 899, the invaders still held the initiative, and it was only under his son, Edward (899–924), that the West Saxons and their Mercian allies went over to the offensive. Nevertheless Alfred not only held the Danes at bay at the crucial juncture; he also prepared the way, by his military measures, for the recovery which followed. These were three: first, a reorganization of the army, creating a mobile force instead of the ineffectual local levies; secondly, the building of a fleet, to fight off the invaders before they made landfall; and, third, the construction of a network of fortified strongpoints, or *burhs*, to provide a backbone for defence. All these were obvious measures to take, and perhaps the most remarkable thing about them, considering the straits in which Alfred found himself in 878, was his ability to put them into effect and to whip up a spirit of resistance in a cowed and defeatist people.

Of Alfred's defensive measures the most striking was the decision to build a fleet. The east Frankish Carolingians, also, had divided up their forces, retaining a mobile contingent under their own control to meet the thrusts of the Magyar cavalry, and Henry I of Germany set up a series of fortified defence-posts along his eastern frontier.[6] But the funda-

48 A twelfth-century English depiction of a landing operation by Danes

mental weakness of the Franks both in the Mediterranean and in the North Sea was the lack of a navy to challenge and beat off the Saracen and Viking marauders. Nevertheless, Alfred's fleet does not seem to have been very efficacious. Quite a number of local victories are recorded, but the raids continued, and it was obviously impossible to safeguard the whole coastline against deft and swift-moving raiders. In the long run, therefore, it was the military measures on land that were decisive, particularly the building of fortified *burhs*, which was carried on after Alfred's death by his son Edward, and his daughter Aethelfled, 'the Lady of the Mercians', as the West Saxons thrust north and east against the lands occupied by the Danes, the so-called Danelaw. It is, in fact, impossible to say with certainty how many of the *burhs* date from Alfred's, how many from Edward's reign; all that is clear is that by the end of Edward's reign there was a chain of fortresses stretching through Wessex and English Mercia, and that they were strategic centres in the struggle for the Danelaw. They were also havens of refuge for the harassed population of the surrounding countryside, and by the middle of the tenth century a number of them were turning into boroughs in the modern sense – i.e. urban settlements and centres of local trade.

This military organization had to be paid for, and the most remarkable success of the West Saxon rulers was their ability to extract the where-withal in the form of work, dues and taxes, from a hard-pressed and war-weary population. The fleet alone was a heavy burden. Even after 1018, when its size was considerably reduced, the wages of the crews have been calculated at £3,000–£4,000 a year, i.e. about what twelfth-century kings received from a levy of Danegeld[7] (i.e. the tribute paid to the Danes to stop their invasions). The cost of building the fleet was laid on the land, each three hundred hides (or peasant holdings) being responsible for one ship. The hides were also the basis of assessment for the upkeep and manning of the *burhs*, and elaborate calculations have been made to show that, a few years after Alfred's death, no fewer than 27,671 men were engaged in garrison duties.[8] However sceptical one may be about the value of such figures, it is obvious that the obligations imposed were heavy, and also that the central concern of the monarchy at this period was to assemble the resources required to maintain the defensive system.

The main evidence for this is the document known as the Burghal Hidage, compiled apparently between 911 and 919.[9] The significance of the Burghal Hidage, as evidence of the administrative arrangements built up in the tenth century, is the way it contrasts with the older Tribal Hidage, through which we can trace the outline of administration as it had been on the eve of the Danish invasions. What we see is that the old tribal or regional framework, visible in the Tribal Hidage, had been swept away, even in Wessex, as a result of the wars, and that its place had been taken by an organization centred upon the fortified *burhs*. Not, of course, that there was a complete breach with the past. Where a royal *villa* or manor-house (a *cinges tuon*) remained, it might be fortified with stockades and earthworks, and continue in its old role as the centre of local administration. But all the evidence suggests that this rarely occurred, and what happened more commonly was that the dues which had flowed earlier from the regions and provinces to the king's tuns, to his reeves in the royal vills, for the upkeep of his household, were now diverted to the upkeep of the fortified *burhs*. Furthermore, the old regional divisions – the lathes of Kent, the rapes of Sussex, the early *scirs* (or shires) of Northumbria and Wessex – had also been swept away as effective units of local government, and the Burghal Hidage, in the area it covers, pays no attention to them. Instead, it simply lists the boroughs of Wessex (and, in addition, the three boroughs of Oxford, Worcester and Warwick), and assigns to each a certain number of hides of land, these lands evidently being charged with the upkeep of the boroughs to which they were assigned.

This rearrangement of dues and services was originally simply a response to immediate, practical needs. Stenton has insisted that it came into being 'for the sole purpose of providing garrisons for the fortresses' and 'gives no ground for any theory that the districts assigned to the fortresses were used as administrative as well as military units'.[10] No doubt he is right for the period at the beginning of the tenth century, of which he is writing. But it is also true that, such administration as existed having been organized round the *burhs*, the organization was used and adapted for other purposes as more settled conditions returned; and that just as the Lombard bishops won control of their cities by taking charge of the city walls and fortifications and maintaining them in good repair, and just as the German dukes asserted their authority in their duchies by their leadership in defence, so the West Saxon kings used the *burhs* they had constructed as centres from which to extend their authority and govern the land. The burghal organization set up orginally for military purposes, became, in short, the basis for a new scheme of local government, which seems to have taken shape in most essentials by the reign of Edgar (959–75).

There are good reasons why this should have been the case. As Jolliffe pointed out, 'the reconquest under Alfred and his sons placed the crown in possession not of a government of England but of the ruins of at least eight national constitutions.'[11] Unlike the Saxon rulers in tenth-century Germany, who could fall back on Carolingian precedent, the kings of Wessex had to start afresh, with the only administrative machinery they possessed, and that was the burghal organization. In the short run, this may have seemed a disadvantage. It meant that, besides reconstituting their own system of government, the kings of Wessex were faced with the task not only of replacing the local units of Sussex, Kent, Essex, Mercia and East Anglia, which had passed out of history, but also of bringing into a common administrative scheme the trithings and wapentakes the Danes had set up in the north and Midlands. On the face of it this was a formidable task. In the longer run, on the other hand, the elimination of the old organization simplified the administrative problems, providing a clear field – one might almost say a *tabula rasa* – when the time came to put through the work of administrative reorganization which the Danish wars had made imperatively necessary. This, no doubt, was what Stenton meant when he wrote that the successful wars of the West Saxon kings against the Danes 'made possible the establishment of a uniform scheme of local administration throughout southern England.'[12]

In detail, the history of this administrative reorganization is obscure, but it was virtually complete by the time of Edgar's death in 975. By that date the shire and hundred organization of later times was in operation, and all the evidence indicates that it was a product of the preceding three-quarters of a century. Chadwick has argued with some force that many of the innovations were taken over or copied from the Danes.[13] This may or may not be the case; but there is no doubt that the Danish boroughs of the Midlands (notably the famous five boroughs of Derby, Leicester, Lincoln, Nottingham and Stafford), which served originally as fortified bases for the Danish armies, became centres of civil government for the surrounding areas after these armies had settled down upon the land, and this basic similarity of organization must at least have facilitated the task of devising a unitary scheme of government for the whole of England after the end of hostilities and the reconquest of the Danelaw. In any case, what we can discern, dimly but surely, is an evolution from the system set out in the Burghal Hidage to the hundred system, or, perhaps more correctly, an adaptation of the burghal organization to peacetime conditions. With the ending of military operations, the burghal districts had served their immediate purpose, and not a few of the *burhs* fell into insignificance, or were even abandoned. In other cases, the burghal districts – that is to say, the areas assigned the task of maintaining the fortified centre – were too large for the purposes of peacetime administration, and were subdivided into hundreds. Nevertheless the borough, where it remained important, retained a key place in the administrative network as the head or centre of the shire. In some instances, perhaps, the shires of the south were put together on the basis, much remodelled, of the primitive settlement areas. But in the Midlands, both English and Danish, a new organization, based on the boroughs, was set up. Oxford, Worcester and Warwick are examples of boroughs that were made heads of shires, and even in Wessex itself the counties of Hampshire and Wiltshire were obviously the districts governed respectively from Southampton and Wilton. Bedford and Northampton are other examples of boroughs older than their shires, which were in effect areas allotted to them for fiscal, military and administrative purposes. In the latter instance, as in the case of Cambridge, this was almost certainly done on the basis of the existing Danish arrangements, for in the Danelaw the shire (as we have seen) was from the beginning the centre of an area occupied and settled by a Danish army.

In the eastern Midlands, therefore, the shire originated in a Danish, in western Mercia in an English, burghal area, and their organization round boroughs is shown, simply enough, by the fact that the shires are named after their boroughs by the addition of a suffix to the name of the principal town. The origins of the hundred are more complicated, and have been the subject of endless controversy. Jolliffe, following Liebermann and Morris, traced its origin to the formation of associations, or groups of one hundred persons, for police duties; while others, including Stubbs, regarded it as a hundred hides of land, apportioned originally to a hundred families.[14] This is not the place to discuss the controversy. The prevalent view, and the one most consonant with the evidence, is that it represented a 'unit of assessment', a method of repartitioning, assessing and collecting dues and services, or what Round called a 'block' for the purpose of 'taxation'.[15] This taxation, from Alfred's time, was for the purpose of maintaining the fortified *burhs*. Then, when peace came, the same method of assessment was used for other purposes. It is here that the origins of the hundred must be sought.

The view of the hundred as an area for the assessment of public burdens also makes it possible to account for the extraordinary discrepancies in the size of hundreds, which, whatever else, did not represent equal divisions of land. According to Liebermann's computations, the area of the hundred varied from one-eighth of a square mile to eighteen square miles. In Cambridge there were 17 hundreds, in Kent 71, in Bedfordshire 9, in Staffordshire 5, but in Sussex 68. One explanation, no doubt, is differences in wealth and population, which particularly affected the north and west.[16] But more important, in all probability, is the greater incidence, in the heart and core of Wessex, where hundreds were small and crowded, of fortified places, and therefore a heavier assessment; whereas as the reconquest moved out farther towards Shropshire and Cheshire, fortified boroughs were less thick on the ground and it was possible to assign their upkeep to a wider area. Moreover, the date at which hundreds and counties were established also clearly made a difference. If Shropshire, for example, was assessed twice as heavily as the adjoining county of Stafford, the reason without much doubt is that Shropshire was added at an early date to the kingdom of Wessex and therefore had to share in the heavy burden of withstanding the Danish onslaught.[17] When the later hundreds were organized in the newly conquered areas, on the other hand, fighting was virtually over, and it was not necessary to exact so big a contribution. In the Danish areas, in particular, in the last phase of territorial arrangement after the victory of Wessex over the Danelaw had been registered, and when military requirements were no longer so pressing, a more or less uniform or 'symmetrical' hundred organization was imposed, and here the assessment approximated closely to the geographical facts – that is to say, the area assessed at a hundred hides actually did contain approximately one hundred hides of land.[18]

The tangled question of the origins of the English shires and hundreds is an intriguing subject for historical speculation. More significant in the long run are two other considerations. The first is that the administrative framework built up in the tenth century marks, with rare possible exceptions, an almost total breach with the past. The first specific mention of the hundred only occurs in the time of Edgar (959–75), and though by then it was evidently an established institution, the earliest date to which it can tentatively be traced is the reign of Edward the Elder (899–924). The shire organization is certainly no older. Except for the name, there is no direct connection between the *scirs* of early Wessex and the shires that meet us there at the end of the tenth century; and elsewhere, notably in the Midlands, the shires are clearly the result of deliberate administrative remodelling. Stenton, almost certainly correctly, attributes their introduction, once again, to Edward the Elder.[19] But the second point is the flexibility and adaptability of the new organization, and its potential as an instrument of government. Although its origins were almost certainly fiscal – that is to say, it provided the king with the means of assessing and collecting dues and services – it could be, and very quickly was, used not only for fiscal but also for judicial and police purposes, and particularly for apprehending thieves. Athelstan, in the ordinance of Grately (*c.* 930), had ordered all men 'belonging to the *burh*' to ride out against anyone who was contumacious and refused to do right. Under Edgar this duty, first imposed on the burghal area, was transferred to the hundred. At the beginning of his famous Ordinance of the Hundred, under the heading: 'That a thief shall be pursued', he enjoins that 'all go forth' and 'do justice on the thief', and this is immediately followed by penalties against the man who fails to take part.[20]

Behind this extension of the sphere of activity of the new hundred organization stood an energetic and powerful monarchy determined to reduce the land to law and order after the upheavals caused by the Danish wars and the lawlessness they had unleashed. Nothing is more remarkable than the spate or ordinances and enactments, from Edward and Athelstan to Edgar and Ethelred, in which the English kings sought to cope with theft – particularly cattle-rustling, which was evidently the most prevalent crime of the age – with overmighty families and kinship groups which flouted the law and 'stood up in defiance of a thief', and with the bands of displaced persons thrown up by the war, 'kinless of paternal relatives', and 'lordless men of whom no law can be got'. This legislative activity was unique in Europe at this time, and we have only to compare it with the helplessness of the west Frankish rulers to gauge the achievement of the Anglo-Saxon monarchy. The hundred organization, which, on the one hand, assured the king of his resources, and, on the other hand, was a potent instrument against the social evils of the day, was an outstanding monument to its effectiveness. The further questions that remain to be answered are: what were the factors or the special circumstances which enabled the Anglo-Saxon rulers to take the initiative in the organization of local government, instead of leaving it, as in France, to the feudal princes, or, as in Germany, to the dukes, and how these rulers succeeded in allocating to local institutions of their own creation tasks and duties, such as the pursuit of thieves, which hitherto had been left to the vengeance of the neighbourhood. How, in other words, did the Anglo-Saxon monarchy come to have such power and authority at a time when elsewhere royal government had either capitulated or, as in Germany, was engaged in a struggle to assert its pre-eminence against a powerful local aristocracy?

THE ANGLO-SAXON MONARCHY

Among the factors making for a strong, energetic monarchy, capable of reorganizing the whole structure of government after the ravages of the Danish wars, the first is that the king's power was based largely on conquest. This fact has already been noted more than once, and there is no need to enlarge on it at length. Outside Wessex, the West Saxon dynasty ruled over lands conquered or reconquered from the Danes. Both in Mercia and in the Danelaw its rights of conquest were a source of strength, since they meant that it did not have to fear the opposition of a 'free' people which laid claim to its own ancient rights and customs. We have seen how this fact enabled Edward to remodel the Mercian administration, ignoring the regions and provinces into which the Mercian kingdom had formerly been divided; and this is only one example of a situation which must have applied elsewhere.

The special position of the king of Wessex as a conquering power is

49 A king sitting with his council; from an eleventh-century English manuscript

expressed in his title. There has been much discussion of the imperial title assumed by the Anglo-Saxon rulers: 'basileus', or 'Bretwalda', or 'king and caesar of all Britain'.[21] What can scarcely be disputed is that it was the title of a conquering dynasty, not of a king raised up by his own people, but of a conqueror who had enforced his dominion over neighbouring peoples and ultimately over the whole island. And it is surely significant that, although the imperial title was in use before the Danish invasions – no doubt as an expression of pre-eminence among the different dynasties of the heptarchy – it was under Athelstan (924–39) that it came to the fore as an expression of the distinctive position of a ruler who had established an overlordship over the whole of Britain, including the Welsh principalities beyond the Wye. Thereafter, until the days of Canute, it is common in royal charters, and its various forms – 'emperor of the Angles and all those races who dwell about them', for example, or 'emperor of the Angles and of the barbarians of this island' – reveal with unusual clarity that it signifies the rule of a conqueror over dependent peoples.

A second factor which favoured the monarchy was that there was no machinery for opposing the king. Much has been written about the 'national assembly' or *witenagemot*, of Anglo-Saxon times,[22] as though there was a formally constituted body from which the king had to secure approval for his acts. This was not the case. Naturally, a sensible king would take care to consult influential people, and only a very foolish 135 king would go against their advice. Moreover, most kings would hold ceremonial courts at festive seasons, at which most influential people would be in attendance. If a king intended something special, such as the promulgation of a new code of law, he would consult appropriate people, and would specifically state, in the prologue to his laws, that they were issued with the advice or assent or consent of his 'wise men'. All this goes without saying. Every ruler, however dictatorial, has his advisers or counsellors, good, bad or indifferent, and in a particular matter or emergency he will enlarge their ranks from the provinces and get together a good-sized assembly. But that is not the same thing as saying that he has to get approval from a formally constituted body, still less that the advisers are representatives of the people. The so-called *witenage-mot*, or assembly of wise men, had no regular meetings. It could not come together unless the king summoned it; and if perchance the magnates thought the king was governing badly or inefficiently and met to discuss a remedy, they were conspiring, and could expect the king, if he got wind of it, to turn up with armed forces and disperse them, if he could. No one had a right to be called to advise the king, and the nearest we can get to a definition of membership is to say that, unless a man were a king's thegn,[23] he would not normally be likely, however rich and powerful he might be, to be summoned to attend. Naturally, a weak king, like Ethelred II (978–1016), would be very much in the hands of his counsellors; but normally, where we get lists of people attending on and advising the king, the solid core was composed of members of the royal family and household, and great churchmen, bishops and abbots.

The support of the church was the third factor strengthening the tenth-century monarchy, and in this respect there is a close parallel between the position of Otto I in Germany and Edgar in England. Archbishop Dunstan had been in exile in Ghent, and there had come into contact with the reforming movements spreading from Brogne and Cluny. He had seen how the great abbots of Cluny, such as Odo and Majolus, looked to the monarchy to help in the work of reform, and when he returned to England, he and his fellow workers, such as Ethelwold of Winchester and Oswald of York, sought to apply to Anglo-Saxon conditions the lessons they had learnt abroad. The result was to cement an alliance or community of interests between the monarchy and the church, which was not new, but which was greatly reinforced, and from which both parties benefited.

The symbol of this new and strengthened relationship in the days of St Dunstan was the introduction of the rite of royal coronation and con-secration, first used at the coronation of Edgar in 973.[24] As early as 787, at a synod held at Chelsea, the Anglo-Saxon king had been called *Christus Domini*, and the same synod issued the programmatic declaration: 'Whosoever resists the royal power is resisting the ordinance of God' and incurring eternal damnation. The new coronation ceremony reinforced the king's transcendental position by adding the solemn rite of unction. The anointing of the king with the sacred oil, with which (in the words of

136

the coronation order) only 'priests and kings and prophets and martyrs' were anointed, raised him out of the ranks of ordinary people, and meant that 'even in the weakest of hands the royal power was upheld by a religious sanction against all other powers in the state.'[25] It also meant, in the eyes of churchmen of that date, that he had a right to direct and interfere in church affairs, to appoint bishops and abbots, and to expect their close co-operation in the work of government. The bishops were leaders not only in the king's council but also in the shires, where they represented royal interests and helped to enforce the king's will.

Even before the introduction of consecration, the king's special position at the head of society had been emphasized by the exaction of an oath of fealty from all men, 'sicut homo debet esse fidelis domino suo'. This oath was imposed by Edmund about 943, and the ability of the West Saxon monarchy to exact it is all the more remarkable when we compare the situation in the Frankish kingdom where, as we have seen,[26] the general oath of fealty had fallen into disuse as early as the middle of the ninth century.

Endowed with this special position in society and buttressed by religious sanctions, the king began to lay claim to certain specifically royal rights, particularly to an overriding interest in the maintenance of peace. The development of the concept of 'the king's peace' is specifically a product of the tenth century. Earlier – indeed, from the time of our earliest records – the king, like anyone else, had his own special peace, and naturally enough it was safeguarded in a higher sum than anyone else's (a 'wite' of 120 shillings as contrasted with a maximum otherwise of 60 shillings for an offence which did not touch the king). Originally, this penalty applied only to the king's person – for example, to fighting in his presence. Gradually it was extended, first to the church, which was under the king's special protection, and fighting in a church incurred the royal 'wite' of 120 shillings; then – already as early as the time of Ine of Wessex (c. 694) – to the royal *burh*, and breach of peace in the royal boroughs was also penalized at 120 shillings. But the significance of these extensions of the king's peace should not be exaggerated. Down to the end of the ninth century – that is, until the end of the reign of Alfred – 'the latent possibilities of kingship remained unrealized'. There were many separate pleas of the crown. The king looked after those specially commended to him, just as any other lord looked after his men, but there was 'as yet no notion of going beyond this to create a special king's law to cover the more dangerous offences.'[27]

From the beginning of the tenth century, this situation began to change, as the monarchy, imbued with the sanctity of divine right, began to assert its prerogatives. Under Alfred – perhaps as a result of inflation – the king's 'wite' went up from 120 sh. to 300 sh., a very heavy penalty indeed. Under Alfred, again, there is the first mention of the 'botless' offence of treason; and this is noteworthy as the first evidence of the heightened conception of kingship which was to be the mark of the tenth century. But the clearest evidence that the monarchy was setting out on a new path was the reconstruction of the whole process of thief-catching, with the duty of pursuit imposed directly on the hundred and enforced by rigid penalties. This has already been discussed.[28] It was by taking in hand the suppression of theft and other evils bred by war and dislocation that the kingship acquired functions differentiating it not only in degree but also in character from all other authorities in the land; it showed that the promise in the king's coronation oath to preserve the church and all Christian men in true peace, was not mere verbiage.

By assuming responsibility for enforcing the peace, the monarchy not only asserted its place at the head of society, but also created new sanctions and a machinery of law enforcement which had not existed before; and as this was a royal machinery, it redounded to the profit of the crown. In particular, the crown broke into the old system of money compensations for theft and other crimes and offences – a system which evidently had broken down under the impact of war, and was no longer effective – and added as a regular process of law the drastic penalty of outlawry. In the course of the tenth century outlawry became a common method of coercion, a penalty for many violent offences. No less important, however, than its extension to a growing range of offences, is the fact that it was the king's punishment, which only he or his officers could invoke. Outlawry was a royal process, and this very fact meant that it placed the final sanction of the law in the king's hands. A second specifically royal process was the ban. Beginning under Edward the Elder – once again, that is to say, in the midst of the period of recovery from the Danish wars – the ban was introduced as a penalty for disobedience of royal orders. Whereas previously the law had been viewed as the custom of the people and the system of fines and mulcts and compensations was incurred for infringements of the customary law, now the king's orders themselves had the force of law, and if the king ordered something to be done, or conversely if he prohibited it, anyone who ignored his orders fell under the ban, with all its consequences.

In these ways and others we can see the crown intervening in the law, improving its procedures by edict, watching over its execution, and punishing those who disregarded or impeded the king's orders. At the same time it was formulating a list of offences – defined early in the eleventh century as 'mundbryce and hamsocn, forsteal and fyrdwite, grithbryce and fihtwite'[29] – which belonged specially to the king's jurisdiction. These special offences are first mentioned under Edgar, whose reign was the high-water mark of the new Anglo-Saxon kingship, and who claimed 'kingship rights in every shire and borough'. They are the rights which are described in the first post-Conquest compilation of Anglo-Saxon law, the so-called *Leges Henrici Primi*, as 'the rights which the king has over all men in his land', and which are described in similar terms in the laws of Canute. As such, they are the starting-point of the later pleas of the crown, and they owe much to the strong rule of Canute who, after a period of decline under Ethelred II, raised the monarchy once again to the peak it had reached under Edgar. It was due to the consolidation of royal power under Canute that, over and above the local laws of Wessex and Mercia and the Danelaw, there rose what the author of the *Leges Henrici* called 'the tremendous empire of the royal majesty'. Royal law, and the royal machinery of law, evolved by the kings of the tenth century from Edward to Edgar, and codified and consolidated by Canute, stood over the old and decrepit codes, and was the main force in government.

But the English kings in the tenth century not only built up a machinery of royal law and royal control of law enforcement: they also saw to it that they had in the provinces a body of servants to watch over and enforce their rights, so that there was no danger of royal policy becoming a dead letter. These servants were the king's thegns, the Anglo-Saxon equivalent of the Carolingian *vassi dominici*, who were the backbone of Carolingian government.[30] Similarly, the king's thegns were the backbone of Anglo-Saxon government. They were the king's 'ministers' or 'administrators' (*ministri* is the word of the chronicles and the Latin charters), and it is impossible to overlook the similarity between them and the German *ministeriales*, on whom the Salian kings of Germany relied for government.[31]

The king's thegns had begun to play a part in local government before the Danish invasions, noticeably in the reign of Ethelwulf (839–58), but it was in the period after the Danish invasions, as a consequence of the military and political expansion of Wessex, that the king's thegns became the principal link between the king and the provincial administration. The thegns owed special obedience to the king, because they were his servants, provided with land in exchange for service, and as such they were compelled, by royal ordinance, to undertake the leadership in the routine of local government – in such things as arrest, hue and cry, pursuit of outlaws. Already at an early date their special position was recognized by a decree ordering that a king's thegn was to be included among the oath-helpers of a man charged with homicide. Before long they developed into a sort of 'legal aristocracy' in control of the local courts. Ethelred, for example, placed the duty of judgment on twelve thegns alone in the Danish areas, and in Wessex also it seems to have been assumed – to judge from the language of surviving official documents – that they were the active element in the shire courts. In addition, of course, they served as the king's messengers and rode on his business. The kings fully recognized their value to them. Edgar specifically promised to maintain them in their lands and status, and Ethelred forbade anyone to exercise jurisdiction over them except the king. As a privileged aristocracy of service (for they appear to have been recruited from all ranks of the free classes, and not all were wealthy or high born), they constituted 'a corps of provincial *ministeriales* more obedient, more at the mercy of the king, and more readily responsive to royal mandates than the Norman kings' – after the Conquest – 'had in their barons'.[32]

Finally, in addition to the body of king's thegns, the shire reeve, or sheriff, makes his first appearance. This was in the reign of Edgar and, as Morris well says, 'The rise of the sheriff, like that of the hundred, fits into a general reorganization of local government consequent on the reconquest of the Danelaw.'[33] The sheriff was essentially a royal official, not, as an older generation of historians once argued, an officer appointed by popular election in the shire court. He continued the tradition of the king's reeves who, in the early part of the tenth century, safeguarded the king's interests from their seats in the royal 'vills' and *burhs*, and he makes his appearance precisely at the time when the burghal areas, which had been the units of government under Alfred and Edward the Elder, were declining in importance and the borough administration, shrinking to its later limits, was being replaced by the system of hundreds and shires. In the new administrative districts, the sheriffs took over the functions – particularly the collection of monies due to the king – which the king's reeves had performed in the burghal areas. But they quickly became more important than the latter (who still, of course, continued to exist in charge of royal estates and royal boroughs), partly as a result of developments in the first half of the eleventh century, when the great provincial magnates, earls and ealdormen, became increasingly independent of the crown, and the sheriff became to all intents and purposes the king's representative in the shire and shire-court and the king's main link with the provincial administration. Most, probably all, were king's thegns; but, as the office developed, they came to stand out among the thegns, with special functions such as the presidency of the shire court. The sheriffs were appointed and removable by the king, and their official character was maintained until the end of the Anglo-Saxon period; in other words, unlike the counts and viscounts in the Frankish realm, they never succeeded (nor is there evidence that they sought to do so) in making their office and position hereditary.

The instrument by which this whole structure of government was articulated and activated was the writ – a short, concise, tersely formulated document, written in the vernacular, which was unique in Europe in its day. The writ was in many respects the most remarkable monument to the efficiency and businesslike qualities of Anglo-Saxon government in the century before the Norman Conquest. The oldest surviving genuine writ dates from the reign of Ethelred II (978–1016), but the use of writs, as a means of transmitting the king's orders, probably reaches back to the reign of Athelstan (924–39).[34] Under Athelstan at any rate, it is clear that an organized writing-office or *scriptorium*, was in existence, staffed in all probability by the clerks of the king's chapel; and only an organization of this sort could have produced the fixed formulas and stereotyped forms which characterize the writ from the very beginning. This, moreover, was the very period when the need for a specific instrument of royal government first began to be felt. During the Danish wars, as Stenton has pointed out,[35] there was an eclipse of written documents of all kinds. Under Athelstan, who set up a new administration in the reconquered southern Danelaw, and to whose reign Liebermann attributed the formation of hundreds, the reorganization of government got under way, and with the reorganization the need for appropriate documentary forms became a matter of urgency. All in all, therefore, we shall not go far wrong if we date the introduction of the writ to the years 925–30, and see it as the final evidence of the revitalization of the monarchy under the sons and successors of Alfred.

FROM ANGLO-SAXON TO ANGLO-NORMAN ENGLAND

By comparison with the situation on the continent of Europe, the achievement of the Anglo-Saxon monarchy in the tenth century was quite outstanding. Germany under the Saxon dynasty made the quickest recovery from the ravages of the invasions; but not even there was there anything remotely comparable to the creation of the hundreds, the organization of the shires, the introduction of the sheriff, the tightening of the machinery of criminal law, the development of an efficient fiscal system, or the invention of the writ. On the other hand, there was in England nothing parallel to the feudal anarchy of France. Though English society from the beginning had been an aristocratic society, with multiple lines of dependence from man to man, and though lordship is in evidence from the time of Ine, the Danish invasions – contrary to what happened in France – did not result in the disintegration of Anglo-Saxon society into a multitude of small feudal fragments.

There has been much debate about Anglo-Saxon feudalism, or the alleged 'trend towards feudalism' in Anglo-Saxon England. All that it is necessary to say is that this trend only becomes significant after 975, when a new wave of Danish invasions, in the reign of Ethelred II, disrupted the work of the West Saxon monarchy. Even so, the effects were mitigated, because Canute, after his succession to the English throne in 1016, used his considerable military power to maintain the system of government he inherited. Nevertheless the rise of the earldoms, which dates from Canute's reign, meant the intrusion of a new element into the political balance, and this new factor was adverse to the crown which, even after the progress during the tenth century, still lacked a local machinery adequate to cope with the great earls, as quickly became apparent in the reign of Edward the Confessor.

Remarkable as was the achievement of the tenth-century kings of England, it would therefore be a mistake to exaggerate their success, as some writers have tended to do. The beginning of a new series of Danish invasions in 980 exposed its limitations and inevitably threw government out of joint. As a new period of unrest and lack of governance assailed the land, many of the king's thegns found it prudent to commend themselves with their estates to the greater provincial magnates, who, particularly for those in outlying regions, were able to provide more effective protection than the king. This was a process similar to that which had undermined the efficacy of the *vassi dominici* in late-Carolingian times,[36] and though the consequences were not so drastic, because the disorders did not go on so long, the result was to deprive the monarchy of one of its main instruments of government. Nor was the   141 weakening of the king's hold over his thegns compensated for by the rise of the sheriff, if only because the sheriff was still less an official than the king's personal representative. There was no machinery behind him, and unless he was backed by a substantial body of king's thegns, he was too weak a link between the king and the shires.

All these factors, combined with the spread of feudal or at least semi-feudal relationships, affected the quality of the late Anglo-Saxon government, particularly in the generation before the Norman Conquest. What is surprising, given the conditions, is how much survived and was carried over intact into the Norman state. The essential administrative divisions of the country – shires, hundreds, and wapentakes – were accepted as a matter of course by the conquerors. The Anglo-Saxon writ was not only taken over by the Norman kings, but was exploited and developed until it became an ordinary instrument of government. In Stenton's words, 'the framework of the Old English State survived the Conquest',[37] and this fact itself is the best testimony to the work of the tenth-century kings who created that framework. England was 'the one western kingdom which had emerged in greater strength from the Danish wars',[38] and it is no exaggeration to say that the reorganization of government under the successors of Alfred was, all in all, the greatest constructive achievement of the tenth century.

50 Page from an Anglo-Saxon manuscript (*c.* 1000) of *Beowulf*

HWÆT WE GARDE

na ingear dagum. þeod cyninga
þrym ge frunon huða æþelingas elle
fremedon. oft scyld scefing sceaþe
na þreatum moneg um mægþum meodo setla
of teah egsode eorl syððan ærest wear
feasceaft funden he þæs frofre geba
weox under wolcnum weorð myndum þah
oð þ him æghwylc þara ymb sitten dra
ofer hron rade hyran scolde gomban
gyldan þ wæs god cyning. ðæm eafera wæs
æfter cenned geong in geardum þone god
sende folce to frofre fyren ðearfe on
geat þ hie ær drugon aldor ase. lange
hwile him þæs lif frea wuldres wealdend
worold are for geaf. beowulf wæs bren
blæd wide sprang scyldes eafera scede
landum in. Swa sceal geong guma gode ge
fe þyrcean fromum feoh giftum on fæder

Nine **The new Europe: promise and problems**

THE LATER YEARS of the tenth and the whole of the eleventh centuries were a period when European society, thrown back and held in check by the incursions of Vikings and Saracens and Magyars, again started to advance. The final check to the invasions came with Otto I's victory over the Magyars in 955 at the battle of the Lech; settled government had been restored to Germany already by this date, and to Italy after 962. These were the preconditions for a new period of progress affecting economic conditions, the political order, culture and religion.

THE SCANDINAVIAN, HUNGARIAN AND SLAV MONARCHIES

Politically, the outstanding feature was the rise of new states on the periphery of the Carolingian world. The emergence of the Scandinavian states, beginning about 900, has already been mentioned;[1] their consolidation went on for the next century, to reach its peak under king Sweyn of Denmark, who conquered both Norway and England, and his son, Canute the Great (1016–35). Canute's empire was the most extensive European state of his day, and he himself, in his relations particularly with the German emperor, played a leading part in the political and diplomatic history of Europe.

But it was in the east, rather than in the north, that the period brought the most far-reaching changes. Here the ending of the Magyar ravages, and of the social and political instability which resulted from them, led to the rapid consolidation of new states. The creation of a Hungarian state by duke Geisa (972–97) and his more famous son, king Stephen (997–1038) has already been noted. Like the Scandinavian kings of the period, Canute and St Olaf of Norway (1015–31), the Hungarian ruler accepted Christianity, and entered into communion with Rome, rejecting the missions from Byzantium; and churchmen coming from the west introduced German political and social practices, so that Hungary was gradually drawn into the ambit of feudal civilization, of which it became, by the thirteenth century, 'the eastern bulwark'.

The establishment of a permanent Hungarian state had lasting and vitally important consequences for the political geography of eastern Europe, since it constituted a permanent bloc, cutting the Slav peoples into two halves, the south Slavs and the north (or, as they are traditionally

51 The four small figures at the bottom right of this illustration from a manuscript edition of St Augustine (*c.* 1200) are Bohemians depicted as inhabitants of the City of God.

52, 53 King Stephen I of Hungary in his coronation robes, and (right) Russians being baptized by missionaries from Byzantium; both details from fourteenth-century manuscripts

called, the west) Slavs. The south Slavs – with the sole exception of the Croats at the head of the Adriatic, whose land became a battleground between east and west – remained henceforward within the orbit of the Roman (or 'Byzantine') empire, from which they acquired their religion and much of their culture; but the northern group, cut off from direct connection with Byzantium, quickly came under the attraction of the west, and all sooner or later adopted the Roman or Latin version of the Christian faith. Here, also, the improved conditions following the settlement of the Magyar invaders in Hungary led, after the defeat in 983 of German attempts to control the whole region as far east as the Vistula, to the welding together of the dispersed Slav tribes into two main states: Bohemia and Poland.

Bohemia had already emerged as a stable political unit under Boleslav I (929–67) in the middle of the tenth century; and although later it was forced into feudal dependence on the German emperor, and its ruler, paying tribute, was counted among the German dukes, he had for all practical purposes unlimited authority within his own land. Already in the eleventh century, he encouraged German settlers, particularly the settlement of merchants in the towns; and although political domination was resisted, the influence of German civilization spread throughout the land.

Poland, more directly affected by German pressure in the time of Otto I, developed somewhat later, but became an independent state under Miesko I (965–92) at the end of the tenth century, and under his son Boleslav Chobry (992–1025) not only maintained this position but sought – unsuccessfully – to build up an empire over the neighbouring Slav peoples. It seems possible that Scandinavian influences may have contributed to bring about the concentration of powers from which the Polish state arose. Certainly these influences played a considerable role in the development of Russia, where Swedish conquerors, moving down

the trade routes from the Baltic to Constantinople, established their hegemony over the native Slavs (the 'eastern' Slavs), founded states at Novgorod and Kiev, and gradually absorbed the intervening lands. By the end of the tenth century, under the great prince Vladimir I (972–1015), they had a foothold on the Black Sea, and had direct relations with Byzantium, from which they received not only Christianity but also the elements of the Graeco-Roman civilization of the Mediterranean.

ECONOMIC RECOVERY

Thus, extending far to the east, the end of the disorders of the invasions saw the rise of a new belt of states, many still relatively primitive, but nevertheless all implying an extension of the sphere of settled government, and in many cases – at least in Poland and Hungary and Bohemia – an extension of the influence of the German empire which Otto I had founded. This extension of settled government resulted in a major change in the political geography of Europe. In Carolingian times, as we have seen, the axis shifted from the Mediterranean to the Rhinelands and north-west Europe. Now there was a further shift, or at least the rise of competing centres of political concentration; and the Carolingian patrimony, once the dominant area, was henceforward only one among a number of centres of power and influence.[2]

The extension of the area of settled government was also important economically; it widened the sphere of commercial exchange; and although the effects were limited to begin with, and perhaps not substantial before the twelfth century, they counted appreciably in the long run. The Scandinavians, though still commonly thought of as plunderers and pirates, were traders on a big scale, though it was in the period of the settled Scandinavian kingdoms that the switch from raiding to trading largely occurred. Across the immense stretches of continental Russia, Scandinavian commerce was linked with the oriental world; and the   147 island of Gothland in the Baltic, where excavations have produced vast hordes of Islamic and Greek coins, appears to have been the great entrepôt for this traffic, and its point of contact with northern Europe.[3] Here the Baltic and eastern trade was linked with that across the North Sea and down the western coast of Europe from Hamburg to Holland and Flanders.

The Scandinavians were too few numerically to retain mastery over this extensive commerce, and in the long run greater importance attaches to the revival of Mediterranean trade, which provided an easier and more direct connection with the east than the overland route across Russia. This revival was a direct result of the restoration of stable government in Italy after Otto I secured control in 962. The end of the long period of civil war and of the struggles for predominance between the great aristocratic families brought about a pacification which was a stimulus both to agriculture and to commerce, which could now move more freely. The consequence was that from the beginning of the eleventh century the maritime cities of Italy took in hand the task of throwing open the Mediterranean to commerce, and of recovering for themselves a place in Mediterranean trade.[4] Venice, since it was founded on the sandy islets of a lagoon where nothing would grow, was driven to commerce, and made it its task to rid the Adriatic sea of Dalmatian pirates. The cities of the western Italian seaboard, particularly Pisa and Genoa, together with Amalfi in the south, directed their efforts to breaking the commercial and maritime predominance of Islam. Passing from defence to attack they drove the Muslims out of Sardinia, and then from about 1015 onwards sought out the Saracens in their harbours, destroyed their fleets and restored security to the Mediterranean.

In part at least, this reversal of fortunes reflects, and was a consequence of, the decline of the Islamic caliphate, which occurred at the very period when Europe, under the Ottonian emperors, was gradually being consolidated. The rise of separate caliphates in Egypt and Spain and subsequent conflicts among the different dynasties, which became more and more accentuated during the tenth century, led to a fractioning of power and, with a new spirit of local autonomy, the growth of small political units which were unable to combine together against the Christians. Thus Sicily, having thrown off the suzerainty of the emir of Africa, broke up into a series of cities at loggerheads among themselves, and became an easy prey for the Normans, who first appeared in the Mediterranean in 1029, called in as mercenaries by the south Italian princes of Benevento, Salerno and Capua, where they rapidly made themselves masters. From this stronghold on the mainland, they turned against Sicily, the conquest of which was completed by 1091, with effects which totally altered the balance of power in the Mediterranean.

Thus the period between 1015 and 1091 saw the growing commercial prosperity of the Italian towns, and with their growing wealth a new accession of strength, which enabled them to extend their authority over the countryside, to absorb and bring under control the counties outside

54 Canute the Great and queen
Emma placing a cross on the
altar of Winchester Abbey;
from a tenth-century manuscript

their walls, and so to make Italian civilization into an urban civilization and Italian government into municipal government.

Nor is there any doubt that Germany and northern Europe derived concrete benefits from this revival of Mediterranean trade. German rule over Italy brought on the one hand a richer culture, on the other a share in a less primitive economy. Through Italy and Burgundy, Germany secured contact with the main trade routes of the early Mediterranean world, which passed from Venice north by the Brenner, and through Lombardy across the western Alps to the fairs of Champagne, where already the Italian and oriental trade met the flow of commerce from the coast of Flanders.[5] This northern commerce was the work of the Vikings when, after the establishment by the end of the tenth century of stable kingdoms, they opened up the northern waters, the North Sea and the Baltic, and from the eastern Baltic penetrated down the trade routes of eastern Europe to Constantinople. In this respect the empire of Canute the Great (1016–35), which united England, Denmark and Norway, constitutes a high-water mark in the revival of commerce. Already by the end of the tenth century, Scandinavian trade brought Flanders into close relations with the North Sea and the Baltic countries.

Yet perhaps even more fundamental was the revival of agriculture as a result of more settled conditions – a revival further stimulated, as commercial expansion got into its stride, by the demand from the towns for agricultural produce, and by the growth of an exchange economy of which it became a part. In Italy, without much doubt, the growing demands of the cities, particularly of the cities of the Lombard plain, were a primary cause of agricultural expansion. Elsewhere, in Germany in particular, the very fact that the restoration of peace and the end of the invasions meant a rising population necessitated more intensive exploitation of the soil. This was manifested primarily in the spread of internal colonization and in land reclamation, the recovery of waste and swamp and forest. In Flanders, progress was such by the middle of the eleventh century that the archbishop of Rheims congratulated count Baldwin V (1035–67) on having transformed regions hitherto unproductive into fertile lands rich with grazing herds.[6] This was accomplished by building dikes and ditches; and major 'public works' (as we may call them) of this character no doubt required the initiative of the prince or of a great and wealthy lord.

For the most part, however, reclamation was the work of the peasantry themselves, who encroached on woodlands and made new arable land. In the east, settlement spread from the valleys into the foothills of the Bohemian and Thuringian forests; and even in the heart of the old colonized land – for example in the Taunus mountains of the Rhineland – new settlements sprang up. Elsewhere, for example in the Black Forest, great noblemen with large tracts of uncultivated land began to offer deliberate encouragement to peasant colonizers by offering them more advantageous terms than their fellow peasants in the long-settled districts – such as the payment of a quit-rent in lieu of predial services – which implied complete or partial enfranchisement from manorial burdens. Thus economic progress inaugurated a new phase of social change, which was of course further stimulated by the new stirrings of town life.

But the most effective means – and the one most used at this period – of bringing an unpopulated or thinly settled area under cultivation, was the foundation of monastic houses; and it was through the widespread foundation of new monastic centres that, in the eleventh century, the work of internal colonization made greatest progress. New monasteries, set up at key-points, directed reclamation in their own interests; and though it is certainly not the only explanation of the spate of new monastic foundations in the eleventh century, the fact that the new houses helped the aristocracy to develop their economic position was without doubt an important factor. 'When a great layman restored or reformed or founded a religious establishment', Ferdinand Lot pointed out, 'it was because he owned it and profited from its revenues.'[7] When Otto I died in 973 there were 108 monasteries in Germany; and probably all of them – thanks to Otto's policy – were firmly attached to the crown. A century later there were over seven hundred, and of these the new foundations, nearly without exception, were 'reformed' houses founded by and dependent upon the aristocracy.

MONASTIC AND RELIGIOUS REFORM

This sudden burst of monastic foundations is another characteristic feature of the new age, the clearest sign of the onset of a new phase of religious, moral and intellectual recovery. For the church, also, had suffered severely from the anarchy which afflicted European society everywhere at the close of the ninth century. The effects of the Carolingian renaissance had worn thin before the ninth century was out; literary production declined again to a trickle, and study fell to a low level; the plight of the monasteries, their lands plundered by the laity, was so bad that they seemed incapable of reforming themselves.[8] The efforts of St Benedict of Aniane, in the time of Louis the Pious, to exclude lay abbots, had only achieved limited success, and were soon forgotten. The monasteries served either as an endowment for royal officials, or for the dynastic purposes of aristocratic families, who used monastic lands to build up their demesnes.

The worse the internal conflicts became in the ninth-century empire, the more the monasteries were used as the resource of the contending parties.[9] And this was particularly the case in the lands of the old Lotharingian 'middle kingdom', where the collapse of authority was greatest, and where the rivalries of east and west had freest play. Of all the regions of Carolingian Europe, Burgundy and the neighbouring lands were those in which the anarchical tendencies of feudalism were most prevalent, and where there was no authority capable of defending the church. By 1016, a few years before the country passed under German rule, the king of Burgundy was a nullity. 'There is no other king who governs thus', wrote a contemporary: 'he possesses nothing but his title and his crown, and gives away bishoprics to those who are selected by the nobles. What he possesses for his own use is of small account; he lives at the expense of the prelates, yet he cannot even defend them or others who are oppressed by their neighbours.'[10]

Such conditions were bound to produce a reaction; and it was scarcely accidental that it was in the lands of the middle kingdom, in Burgundy and Lorraine, that a reform movement sprang up almost at the moment of greatest decline. This movement was the reaction of the church, which suffered most from the anarchy, to the ills which secular society had proved itself incapable of remedying.[11] It was essentially a monastic movement, because everywhere the bishops were caught up, in the spirit of Carolingian government, in affairs of state. And it owed much to the piety of a few great noblemen, who took the initiative in founding new monastic houses, reformed houses, the lives of whose inmates were intended to be a reproach to the monks in the older secularized foundations.

Most famous of the reformed monasteries is Cluny, founded in 910 by duke William of Aquitaine in a remote corner of the duchy of Burgundy, some fifteen miles beyond the borders of the Burgundian kingdom. But Cluny was only one of many centres active in the revival of monastic life. Almost contemporary – it was founded in 914 – was Brogne in the duchy of Brabant, which became the main centre of reform for the diocese of Liège. Thence it spread southwards to Gorze, near Metz, which was reformed in 933, and in the next generation the 'Gorzean' reform penetrated slowly up the valley of the Moselle. The famous abbey of St Maximin at Trier was also affected, and St Maximin carried the movement into the diocese of Cologne, where old houses were reformed and new reformed houses, such as Gladbach, were founded.

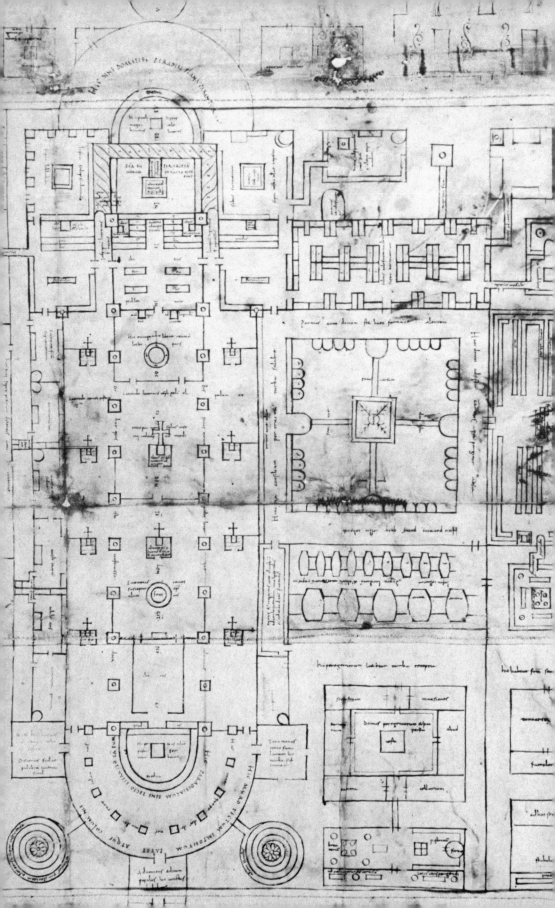

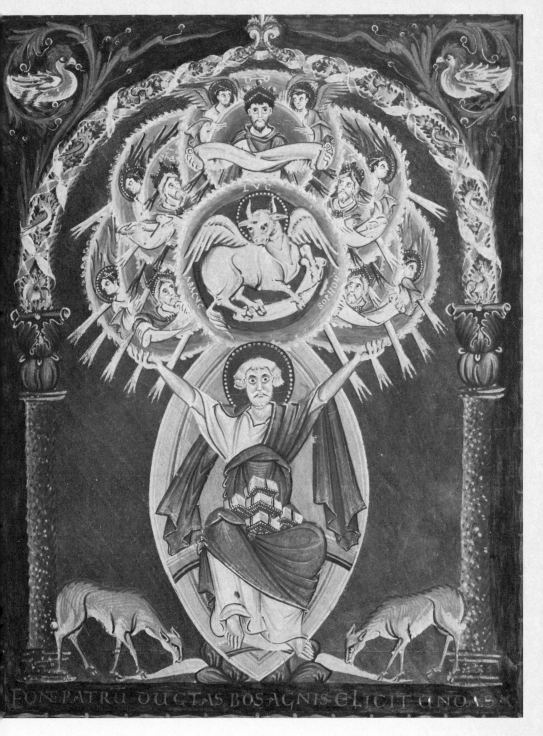

FONS PATRU DUCTAS BOS AGNIS ELICIT UNDAS

55 Detail from the famous ideal plan drawn up for the Benedictine monastery of St Gall (ninth century)

56 An illumination from the Gospels of Otto III (983/1002)

The Saxon rulers of the tenth century paid little attention to the reform movement; it was only later, in the eleventh century, that it secured royal patronage. But the restoration of stable conditions by Otto I was a decisive factor in facilitating its spread; and it soon extended through the middle to the upper Rhinelands. Sometime between 929 and 934 the famous abbey of Einsiedeln was founded; and from Einsiedeln, St Wolfgang – at first a missionary in Hungary, and then bishop of Regensburg – carried the movement into Bavaria, planting the seeds of reform in Bavarian monasteries such as Tegernsee and Niederaltaich and reforming the old house of St Emmeram in Regensburg. From here it spread northwards into Saxony. New centres of study, like the monastic school of St Emmeram and the episcopal school of Bamberg, became from the start of the eleventh century connecting links between north and south, collecting recruits and spreading culture in all regions of Germany. St Godehard, who became bishop of Hildesheim in 1022, carried the reform into Saxony, and helped to raise Saxony to the same level of civilization as Swabia and Bavaria. Meanwhile, Cluny itself was carrying out the reform of centre after centre of monastic life in a widening circle spreading from Burgundy into Aquitaine, to Normandy and England, and south into Italy. The reform of the English church by St Dunstan was inspired both by Brogne and by Cluny.[12]

It would be difficult to exaggerate the importance of these reform movements in changing the tone of society after the middle of the tenth century. In Germany, the revived monasticism was an important factor, politically, in breaking down regional differences – particularly the difference between north and south – in imposing a uniform civilization and creating (what hitherto had been lacking) a sense of common German identity.[13] The revival of discipline also resulted in a revival of literary and artistic life, especially in the sphere of the Lorraine reform movement; so that once again we are confronted with distinguished intellectual personalities such as Notger and Wazo of Liége. Cluny itself was not outstanding in this regard;[14] its distinctive feature was the high degree of organization it achieved and the organizing ability of its abbots, which enabled it to ride out the perils to which other less organized congregations succumbed. The autonomy and independence characteristic of early Benedictine monasticism were not adequate for times of anarchy and disturbance. They left each individual monastic establishment isolated and a prey to the neighbouring feudality. The Cluniac reform was the first successful effort to give homogeneity and compactness to a monastic system, which itself had succumbed, like all else, to the stress and strain of the period of Viking and Saracen invasion.[15]

This, it is true, had not been the case from the beginning. Direct control over the dependent houses – the characteristic feature of Cluniac organization – was only achieved step by step, and appears to have been largely the work of St Odilo (990–1049). He rejected the system of isolated, independent monasteries: only a powerful centralization could save them from the influence of the secular world. Therefore the head of

57 St Dunstan, reformer of the English church, at the foot of the Virgin Mary; detail from a tenth-century manuscript

the community was invested with plenary powers: he was not only absolute master in his own house, but governed all the houses founded by the order. All monasteries founded or reformed by Cluny were directly dependent on it. There was only one abbot, namely the abbot of Cluny, and only one monastery, namely the monastery of Cluny. The rest were affiliated houses, cells or priories, whose heads were not elected by the inmates but nominated by the abbot of Cluny. Similarly the ruling abbot chose his own successor before his powers began to fail through age. In this way a centralized 'monarchical' organization was built up, in which unity was further assured by regular visitations of the dependent priories and by the holding at Cluny of 'chapters-general', which the priors had to attend. The contrast between this hierarchical organization and the independence of every Benedictine monastery from the others was fundamental. It was the adaptation of feudal practices and methods to monastic organization, the conveyance of feudal ideas of lordship, homage, service and fealty into the cloister.[16] The abbot of Cluny was a 'grand suzerain'. Cluniac monasticism was the reply of the church to feudal disorganization, 'the feudal system minus the looseness and particularism of that system'; and it made Cluny a major power in the feudal world.

GATHERING STORMS

In the sphere of religion, as in that of politics, the century after 955 thus saw the rise of a new power – the power we associate with the name of Cluny. The restoration of peace and stability by the Ottonian dynasty released new forces. But these forces, which could scarcely have come into existence without the Ottonian achievement, were fatal to the structure of government which they built. Thus after the period of the invasions, out of which the German monarchy arose as the strongest power because it retained most of the Carolingian inheritance, we reach the threshold of a new period, in which this revived Carolingian government – already archaic and backward-looking – was undermined and finally destroyed. This new period begins at the end of the eleventh century. But the seeds of the new are in the old, and from the beginning of the eleventh century we can perceive the gathering of storm clouds. Every aspect of progress, political, economic, religious, created new problems; and when those problems matured and were merged together, the crisis broke.

Politically, in the first place, the consolidation of new kingdoms in the east created new complications for the German rulers. It is unnecessary to discuss in detail the relations between Germany and Poland, Bohemia and Hungary in the eleventh century – although, as has rightly been said, it was the decisive, formative period in the history of central Europe, when 'the foundations of the following centuries were laid'.[17] Suffice it to say that, so long as they were confronted by small divided Slav tribes, the problems of the eastern frontier were not serious for the German rulers, and the reign of Otto I had seen great progress in Germanization at Slav expense. But from the beginning of the eleventh century, when Germany came face to face with consolidated states in the east, the picture changed. Henry II saw himself confronted from the beginning of his reign in 1002 by a Polish power which not only threatened to regain the lands in the east occupied in the previous century, but which, by linking up with Bohemia, looked as though it might form a Slav state 'able to deal with Germany on equal terms'. Rightly or wrongly, he determined to act, and allying with the heathen Slavs, he attacked Poland in 1005. It was the first of the many conflicts between Germany and Poland.

Thereafter, throughout Henry II's reign and that of his successor Conrad II, and of Conrad's son, Henry III, the eastern frontier was scarcely ever at peace. Hungary also was involved, both under St Stephen and after his death in 1038. After the first Polish campaign of 1005 another followed in 1010, another in 1015, a further campaign in 1017; Conrad II was at war with both Poland and Hungary in 1030 and 1031; Henry III attacked Bohemia in 1040 and Hungary in 1043 and 1044. It was, one may say, a running sore, for military victory led to no final results. And inevitably it diverted the emperor's attention from Italy and Germany, particularly from the western frontier where Lorraine, never so securely held as the German parts of the realm, became an increasingly serious problem. That in these circumstances Germany was able to conquer the kingdom of Burgundy in 1034 is remarkable. But in the long run it became more than was possible to maintain hegemony in both east and west, and the result of the complications on the eastern frontier was the gradual loosening of control over Lorraine, where from 1044 duke Godfrey was a thorn in Henry III's side.

Italy also was affected. In particular the occupation of Sicily and lower Italy by the Normans went ahead without German intervention, and all Conrad II and Henry III could do was to attempt to win over the Normans by recognizing their tenure and playing upon their hostility to the Roman empire in the east, whose lands they had occupied. Nevertheless, here also was a new power, still friendly, but potentially dangerous. On every frontier – even in the north where Canute the Great had built his

58 Polish soldiers; detail from an eleventh-century silver bowl

wide-flung empire – the German ruler had new powers to face, powers which felt German preponderance as a threat, and might, almost at a moment's notice, be mobilized against the emperor.

If such was the position externally, the internal position was equally precarious. In Italy, the economic revival had played into the hands of the knights in the countryside, who were determined to throw off feudal bonds in order to exploit their lands more freely. In the towns, it was already leading to antagonism between the commercial classes, who wished to direct civic affairs in their own interests, and the bishops, whom the Ottonian settlement had left in control of the cities. And these two sources of opposition frequently coalesced, for the knights were in large part vassals of the bishops, and their policy also was anti-episcopal.

157

59 Henry II of Germany (1002–24) holding a jewelled Gospel; eleventh-century manuscript

60 Emperor Conrad II and his son, Henry III; stained-glass window in Strasbourg cathedral

Thus in Italy the restoration of order and the consequent economic progress set in motion a social revolution, the rise to power of new classes in the population and their struggle to better their position against the existing authorities. But because German government relied on the bishops, this social revolution turned into a political revolution directed against the German government, and even took on the hue of an Italian national movement. When Otto III died in 1002, the Italians elected an Italian king, marquess Arduin of Ivrea; or rather an Italian party elected a king for themselves, for Arduin represented essentially the interests of the lesser nobility, the *secundi milites*, knights or vavassours, against the great dukes and the bishops. Already the cities (for example, Cremona) were seeking to get into their own hands the comital rights and control of markets, tolls, minting of coinage, etc. which the Ottonian kings had confirmed to the bishops; already the knights in the countryside were trying to secure free disposal of their lands, rejecting the rights of their overlords, seeking to free themselves from dependence; while the great lords and bishops, because of the increased chances of profit, were clinging ever more strongly to their seignorial rights over waste and commons and seeking to prevent their free exploitation by their tenants.

Arduin was quickly subdued, once the new German king, Henry II, fully occupied at first on the Polish frontier, was able to intervene; but the social antagonisms in Italy continued to gather force under the surface, and finally came to a head in the great revolt of the vavassour class, the Italian civil war of 1035. In 1042–43, this was followed by bitter civil war in Milan, this time between nobles and non-nobles.

Finally, the social agitation merged with the reform movement in the church, which provided an unequalled pretext for opposition not only to the bishops but also to German rule. By attacking the right of the German ruler to appoint the bishops, which was now denounced.as 'simony', the reformers cut away the ground from beneath both the episcopacy and the imperial government. Milan soon became the centre of the new movement, which spread quickly throughout Lombardy, and had the support of all parties which hoped to profit from a dissolution of the existing order in church and state. The new movement got the nickname 'Pataria', i.e. the rag-pickers; but it was not, as used to be thought, a movement of the 'ignorant lower classes', the rabble.[18] On the contrary, its main support came from the knights and the middle classes of the towns; for the programme of free elections was in their interests, as much as it was against those of the government. So far as the German government was concerned, it meant the end of any possibility of influencing and controlling Italian affairs by nominating prelates it could trust to the episcopal sees – which meant, in fact, to control of the cities. So far as the bishops were concerned, it meant the end of any attempt to maintain their rights against the twofold attack of their feudal tenants and the citizens. For 'free election', in the sense in which the phrase was used at that time, meant the election of the bishop by the clergy and people of the church; that is, in practice, the choice by the knight class and by the cathedral clergy, who were recruited from the knightly families, of one of themselves.

Such elections could only mean the end of episcopal authority, a surrender to the claims and agitation of the episcopal vassals; and the prelates rallied behind the archbishop of Milan, who brought together a synod and condemned the Pataria. But in 1056 the pope annulled the archbishop's excommunication of the leaders. Thus the Pataria was formally recognized by the papacy, which had its own reasons for wishing to break the power of Milan, the see of St Ambrose, which was at that time the leading church of Italy. In this way the stage was set for a major conflict, in which the whole constitution of Italy would be revolutionized. In any case it was easier to condemn the new movement, and to place it under an anathema, than to destroy it, for it rested on irresistible social and economic forces, and in the final analysis the issue could only be resolved by force.

If by 1056 there were in Italy all the elements of revolution, in Germany also events were moving more slowly in a similar direction. Here too economic recovery favoured elements which, in the final analysis, were hostile to the government – namely, the aristocracy which, from 955, the imperial government, with its growing reliance on the bishops, had held more and more at arms' length. Inevitably the aristocracy in these circumstances concentrated increasingly on the development of its own economic resources; and there is no doubt that the economic revival which we have seen, the colonization and opening up of new land, mainly fell to its profit.

It is not easy to trace step by step the growing power of the German aristocracy in the second half of the tenth and the first half of the eleventh centuries; it was a process which went on, so to say, under the surface. But a number of factors may be picked out.[19] First, there was the weakness of feudal bonds in Germany, the lack of a clearly stratified feudal hierarchy. This, without doubt, had been one of the causes of the failure of the German dukes in their struggle with the crown. Unlike the French princes, they were not feudal lords; and therefore they could not use feudal rights to consolidate their position. Thus whereas in France the growth of feudalism resulted in the subjection of the nobility in a feudal hierarchy under the princes, in Germany the old free aristocracy survived with its rights unimpaired, just as did the free peasantry, in Saxony in particular. And the survival of a free class, noble and peasant, meant the survival of free or 'allodial' land, which gave the nobility a solid basis of material wealth on which to base their attitude of independence.

In Germany, therefore, the free classes remained free, and jealous of their liberty; vassalage, in France the mark of a free man, was regarded in Germany as a degrading servitude. Secondly, this strong sense of liberty, of the inherent rights of the free nobility, increased rather than diminished as a result of the struggle between the crown and the dukes in the tenth century. The very preoccupation of Henry I and Otto I with the duchies left the aristocracy free to develop its position; the success of the monarchy in restricting the powers of the dukes meant that the lesser nobility, unlike that of France and Italy, was never subjected in the same way to firm superior control. Intermediate authority, equivalent to that exercised by the French princes, was weak, if not entirely lacking; the monarchy, on the other hand, could not muster the means and the administrative machinery to exercise direct control throughout the length and breadth of Germany. The counts could control the small peasant freemen on behalf of the crown; but over against the great aristocratic families, from whose ranks they were themselves chosen, and who were their social equals, their position inevitably was less secure; indeed the aim of the aristocracy was to obtain over their own lands and dependants the same rights and powers, excluding the count, as the count exercised over the peasantry on behalf of the crown. Thus it may be said that the success of the Ottonian dynasty in dealing with the dukes hid a more fundamental weakness – namely, the failure to reduce the independence of the aristocracy.

This became evident when the development of the reform movement altered the balance of power in favour of the aristocracy. The Ottonian dynasty had restored, and relied upon, royal control over the church. But the vast majority of new monastic foundations in the century after Otto I's death – well over five hundred houses, increasing the number of monasteries about sixfold – were, as we have seen, foundations of the aristocracy, set up for the main part on their allodial estates, and free from direct royal control. In this way the unity of the German church, as one national church under the control of the king and therefore an instrument of royal policy, was destroyed; and the aristocracy got a new accession of power, when, through the gifts of the faithful, their foundations came into possession of more and more lands. In this respect, Cluniac precedent served them well. Just as William of Aquitaine had placed Cluny directly under the Holy See, so the German aristocratic founders placed their houses under papal protection – thus excluding the protection of the king – and in return the papacy granted them rights of advocacy, that is to say, the right to protect and direct the secular relationships of the protected house, including rights of jurisdiction over its tenants. This arrangement dates from the pontificate of Leo IX (1048–54), himself a south German aristocrat, and was a turning-point; for although Leo IX's own relations with the emperor Henry III remained amicable to the end, the underlying implication of a community of interests between the papacy and the German aristocracy against the imperial government was there, ready to be demonstrated in an emergency.

The first signs that an emergency was brewing were already becoming evident before the death of Henry III in 1056. It arose from the fact that the German rulers of the eleventh century, aware of the great economic revival which was taking place, themselves made every effort to profit from it. The Saxon dynasty had become extinct in 1024, and was succeeded by a new line: the Salian dynasty, whose strength, unlike that of the Saxons, lay in the south-west, where progress in agrarian development was more marked than in the Saxon north. The kings of the new dynasty, Conrad II (1024–39), Henry III (1039–56) and his son Henry IV (1056–1105), were aware of the need for new administrative methods more in harmony with the changed social and economic conditions than those inherited from Otto I. In particular, they gave greater attention to the husbanding of their resources, to the better administration of the royal estates, to the reassertion of royal rights and dues, and the recovery of crown lands and forest which had been encroached upon and expropriated. For this purpose they drew, from the ranks of their unfree dependants, a new class of administrators, known as *ministeriales*, who quickly rose in importance, drew apart from the main body of ordinary servile tenants, and became the main agents of royal policy.

The *ministeriales* had probably first been employed by bishops on episcopal estates and the Salians may have seen the advantages. At any rate, it seems that Conrad II was the first German ruler to favour them as a class, and to organize them as a sort of administrative staff.[20] Werner, his chief *ministerialis*, was the earliest secular minister in the history of Germany; in his capacity as supervisor of the 'fisc' (or royal estates) he was a kind of comptroller-general. Even more notable was Benno, who rose rapidly in the service of Henry III, became mayor of the imperial palace at Goslar, chief administrator of the crown lands, and was appointed to the bishopric of Osnabrück in 1054 – an appointment which marks the first breach in the hitherto essentially aristocratic constitution of the German church. But this policy of employing and preferring *ministeriales* almost of necessity alienated the aristocracy, and brought aristocratic opposition to a head. Already in the last years of Henry III hostility to the new administrative policy of the monarchy was becoming visible, and after his death in 1056, when for ten years government passed into the hands of a regency, the opposition of the aristocracy to the *aulici administratores* was loud and violent. When the chroniclers after 1056 complain that the king is surrounded by *vilissimi et infimi homines*, that he listens only to low-born counsellors and spurns the advice of high-born princes, they are voicing the aristocracy's complaints against the new tendency of the monarchy to rely on the *ministeriales*.

THE BIRTH OF A NEW ERA

Thus in Italy and in Germany by 1056 political storms were brewing. In addition, the reform movement which Henry II and Henry III had fostered turned against the crown. There has been a great deal of debate about the causes of this cleavage, and particularly whether the reformers, above all the Cluniacs, had political interests and a political programme. Some writers have argued that Cluny was interested only in moral reform, in raising the standards of monastic life; and far from being concerned with the laity, was not even interested in the secular clergy: 'A profound error', says Abbé Berlière;[21] and with his judgment we may concur. Reform was not, and could not be, a purely monastic affair; for it was clear enough that the objective of freeing the monasteries from secular influences never would, nor could, be firmly accomplished, unless and until lay society was purified from the evils of feudal violence, and particularly until society was at peace within itself. Hence, beside the programme of free election (*electio libera*), i.e. to free the churches (particularly the monastic churches) from lay control, Cluny set out to raise the standard of lay society by direct action, and above all to eradicate the worst excesses of feudalism.

From the last decade of the tenth century, beginning with the synod of Narbonne in 990, numerous synods were called together, in which leadership was in the hands of Cluniac abbots and bishops, at which sanctions were promulgated against thieves, violators of sanctuary and despoilers of church properties, and in which the church extended its protection to merchants and peasants. The movement started in the lands of the middle kingdom, where anarchy was at its worst; it was a remarkable example of spontaneous co-operation against evils which those nominally in authority had proved unable to remedy. And the most remarkable feature was the success in securing the co-operation of the feudatories themselves. If it was only rarely possible to persuade the nobility to forswear private war altogether, it was much easier to get them to limit its exercise; and in this way the idea of the *Treuga Dei*, the truce of God, was born. But the reformers did not stop there. They also sought active as well as passive co-operation, persuading the barons, where necessary, to help with arms in enforcing the peace. Thus the idea of war in a holy cause, of holy war – the idea from which the crusades originated – was born from the peace movement, which rapidly spread both east and west. By 1047 the peace of God had spread to Normandy, by 1063 to Flanders; in Germany it had great influence over the ideas and actions of the emperor Henry III.

There was, at this stage, no fundamental conflict between the aims of the reformers and those of the monarchy. The king, with his sense of divine mission and ministry, with his royal prerogatives which elevated him above the laity, and indeed to further his interests, was the most likely ally of the reformers in their attempts to free the churches from the control of the lay aristocracy. This was particularly true of the emperor Henry III.

Henry III had no hesitation in using his royal powers to reform the church and the papacy, and his actions met with general approval. No one doubted his conscientiousness, his good faith, his deep religious sense. But the approval was rather for his personal merits than for a system which gave ultimate control of the church to the ruler; and already there was a sense alive that, in the hands of another, what Henry did for the good of the church might become an intolerable abuse. The idea

that it ran counter to the spirit of the church for the emperor to nominate

61 Henry III; from an Evangelium (*c.* 1040) which bears his name

bishops and abbots, and even the pope, was beginning to dawn in the minds of a few more inquiring spirits, such as Siegfried of Gorze, Wazo of Liége, Abbo of Fleury; but most people still took the view that, considering the unsettled conditions of the time, this was a necessary state of affairs. For the majority, indeed, it was part of the divine dispensation; the king was no layman; he was king and priest, *rex et sacerdos*, 'mediator' between clergy and people, in whom God's ruling will was operative; and the pope himself had asserted that according to the ancient custom of the church, the king alone had the right to appoint bishops. Nevertheless, the first seeds of doubt were there before Henry III's death in 1056. Custom was one thing, law another; and it was not long before law and custom would come into conflict.

The conflict came to a head through three things, two fundamental and one merely incidental. Incidental was the weakening of the position of the German monarchy after Henry III's death in 1056, when his son Henry IV was a minor; government passed into the hands of a weak regency, and became a nullity, allowing free play to all the incipient tendencies to the dissolution of existing social bonds. Fundamental were, first, the carrying of the reform movement to Rome, and secondly the linking-up – in a unique but remarkable chain of circumstances – of the various disturbing quasi-revolutionary (or should one say proto-revolutionary?) developments outlined above. The result was the sudden crystallization of a broad revolutionary front. The opposition of this unified revolutionary front brought down the old order – the order which we associate with the restoration of the empire by Otto I in 962 – and ushered in, after a generation of conflict, a new period of history in which the forces at play, shaped and moulded in the course of the conflict, were different from before. Indeed the conflict which ensued between 1073 and 1122 may be compared to the upheaval caused by the ninth-century invasions: the latter were the solvent of Carolingian society, the events of the half-century after 1073 the solvent of the society arising out of the invasions. By 1122 European society had another shape, another centre, another content; and European history set out on new paths.

Notes on the text

One: Prelude to Charlemagne

1 G. Barraclough, *European Unity in Thought and Action* (Oxford 1963) 7–10; D. Hay, *Europe. The Emergence of an Idea* (Edinburgh 1957) 116–17
2 R. H. Bautier, *The Economic Development of Medieval Europe* (London/New York 1971) 18–39
3 R. Latouche, *The Birth of the Western Economy* (New York/London, 2nd ed. 1967) ix
4 H. Pirenne, 'Un contraste économique: Mérovingiens et Carolingiens', *Revue belge de philologie et d'histoire*, II (1923) 223–35
5 C. Dawson, *The Making of Europe* (London 1932) 284–86
6 W. Gordon East, *An Historical Geography of Europe* (London/New York, 5th ed. 1966) 151–53, 231–32

Two: The Carolingian legacy

1 H. Fichtenau, *Das karolingische Imperium* (Zürich 1949) 32, 42
2 See below, p. 136
3 E. Hoffmann, 'Knut der Heilige und die Wende der dänischer Geschichte im 11. Jahrhundert', *Historische Zeitschrift*, CCXVIII (1974) 529–70
4 M. Defourneaux, *Les Français en Espagne aux XIe et XIIe siècles* (Paris 1949)
5 Ferdinand Lot, *La Fin du monde antique et le début du moyen âge* (Paris 1927) 469
6 Fichtenau, *op. cit.*, 39
7 *Ibid.*, 45
8 H. von Schubert, *Geschichte der christlichen Kirche im Frühmittelalter* (Tübingen 1921) 636
9 This argument was advanced, perhaps with some exaggeration, by H.-X. Arquillière, *L'Augustinisme politique* (1934); whatever reservations one may have about Arquillière's formulations they do not detract from its essential truth.
10 *Cf.* J. W. Thompson, *The Dissolution of the Carolingian Fisc* (Berkeley/Cambridge 1935), an excellent monograph, which has been undeservedly neglected.
11 F. L. Ganshof, *The Carolingians and the Frankish Monarchy* (London/Ithaca 1971) 247–48
12 Fichtenau, *op. cit.*, 186–87
13 *Ibid.*, 189
14 *Ibid.*, 255–56
15 E. Pfeil, *Die fränkische und deutsche Romidee des frühen Mittelalters* (Munich 1929) 135–37
16 *Ibid.*, 124
17 Alcuin, *Epist.* 174; see Heldmann, *Das Kaisertum Karls des Grossen* (Weimar 1928) 62–63
18 von Schubert, *op. cit.*, 384–85
19 Accepted by Lot, Pfister and Ganshof, *Les Destinées de l'empire en occident de 395 à 888* (Paris 1940–41) I, 478
20 *Ibid.*, 479
21 Heldmann, *op. cit.*, 309, n. 1. Lot, *La Fin du monde antique*, 296, described it, more caustically, as 'a comedy improvised by a handful of antiquarian-minded ecclesiastics'.
22 Halphen, *Charlemagne et l'empire carolingien* (Paris 1947) 137, 138
23 The annals of Lorsch; see *Ann. Lauresheim* (ed. Pertz) 38, (ed. Katz) 34
24 We may safely ignore the case of Louis II in 871, reported only in the Chronicle of Salerno (Cap. 107); it has a special explanation.
25 Heldmann, *op. cit.*, 385 n. 4, 387, 391 ff.
26 *Ibid.*, 421–23
27 Ganshof, *op. cit.*, 244–45
28 Lot, Pfister and Ganshof, *op. cit.*, 480
29 Halphen, *op. cit.*, 136
30 Fichtenau, *op. cit.*, 192

Three: The decline and fall of the Carolingian empire

1 J. Calmette, *L'Effondrement d'un empire et la naissance d'une Europe, IXe-Xe siècles* (Paris 1941)
2 P. Lehmann, *Das literarische Bild Karls des Grossen, vornehmlich im lateinischen*

Schriftum des Mittelalters (Munich 1934)

3 See above, p. 26

4 J. Goebel, *Felony and Misdemeanor* (New York 1937) 132

5 *Ibid.*, 124

6 R. Poupardin, 'Les grandes familles comtales à l'époque carolingienne', *Revue historique*, LXXII (1900) 72 ff.

7 Lot, Pfister and Ganshof, *Les Destinées de l'empire*, 576

8 Ganshof, *The Carolingians and the Frankish Monarchy*, 259

9 Fichtenau, *Das karolingische Imperium*, 117

10 J. Calmette, *Le Monde féodal* (new ed., Paris 1951) 162

11 Halphen, *Charlemagne et l'empire carolingien*, 239–40

12 *Ibid.*, 241

13 *Ibid.*, 226

14 *Ibid.*, 498

15 There were many cross-currents which obscured the conflict of principle, but this was the fundamental basis of alignment; see H. von Schubert, *Geschichte der christlichen Kirche im Frühmittelalter*, 397–98.

16 *Ibid.*, 403

17 *Ibid.*, 410

18 Heldman, *Das Kaisertum Karls des Grossen*, 433–35

19 As is rightly emphasized by Calmette, *Le Monde féodal*, 110

20 Fichtenau, *op. cit.*, 220–21, 223

21 Lot, Pfister and Ganshof, *op. cit.*, 523

22 Calmette, *Le Monde féodal*, 113

23 Lot, Pfister and Ganshof, *op. cit.*, 536

24 *Ibid.*, 512

25 Calmette, *Le Monde féodal*, 113

26 *Ibid.*, 114

27 *Cambridge Medieval History*, III, 28

28 Heldmann, *op. cit.*, 437, 434

Four: The impact of invasion

1 *Cambridge Medieval History*, III, 62

2 Calmette, *Le Monde féodal*, 118

3 Their impact is nowhere better summarized than by Bloch, *La Société féodale* (Paris 1939–41), I, Part I

4 Fichtenau, *Das karolingische Imperium*, 254

5 *Ibid.*, 239

6 Lot, Pfister and Ganshof, *op. cit.*, 578

7 Tellenbach, *Königtum und Stämme in der Werdezeit des deutschen Reiches*, 13–14

8 Fichtenau, *op. cit.*, 117

9 Goebel, *op. cit.*, 131–32

10 See above, p. 76

Five: Feudal France

1 The following account draws on the literature on feudalism listed below,

p. 172, particularly on F. L. Ganshof, *Qu'est-ce que la féodalité?* (2nd ed. Neuchâtel 1947), H. Mitteis, *Lehnrecht und Staatsgewalt* (Weimar 1933), and L. Reynaud, *Les Origines de l'influence française en Allemagne* (Paris 1913). It seems unnecessary to make more detailed references.

2 F. Lot, *Études sur le règne de Hugues Capet* (Paris 1903) 216

3 Migne, *Patrologia latina*, CXXXIII, 660–61; Mitteis, *op. cit.*, 268

4 Calmette, *Le Monde féodal*, 168

5 The process is discussed in general by Lot, Pfister and Ganshof, *Les Destinées de l'empire*, I, 578; the position in Flanders is discussed more specifically by Pirenne, *Histoire de Belgique*, I (3rd ed., Brussels 1909), F. L. Ganshof, *La Flandre sous les premiers comtes* (2nd ed., Brussels 1944), and J. Dhondt, *Les Origines de la Flandre et de l'Artois* (Arras 1944).

6 Mitteis, *op. cit.*, 191

7 *Ibid.*, 169

8 *Ibid.*, 50–51

9 Mitteis, *op. cit.*, 174; Bloch, *op. cit.*, I, 300; Ganshof, *Féodalité*, 73; Fustel de Coulanges, *Institutions politiques de l'ancienne France*, VI, 427

10 This was the view propounded, for example, by J. Flach, *Les Origines de l'ancienne France*, I (Paris 1886); see also G. Monod, *Du rôle de l'opposition des races et des nationalités dans la dissolution de l'empire carolingien (Annuaire de l'école des hautes études*, Paris 1895).

11 It has, however, recently been resuscitated, in a modified form, by W. Keinast, *Der Herzogstitel in Frankreich und Deutschland* (Munich 1968). J. Dhondt, *Études sur la naissance des principautés territoriales en France* (Bruges 1948) 244–47, adopts a middle position. There was, he says, 'a national element at the base of the principalities', but none was really national, and the use of the old pre-Carolingian names (Burgundy, etc.) is deceptive: conquest made the prince.

12 Reynaud, *op. cit.*, 35

13 Mitteis, *Der Staat des hohen Mittelalters*, 136

14 It is worth emphasizing, nevertheless, that a book such as L. Halphen, *Le Comté d'Anjou au XIe siècle* (Paris 1906), tells us more about the reality of eleventh-century France than can possibly be gathered from general accounts of French history.

15 Bloch, *op. cit.*, I, 303

16 *Ibid.*, 266

17 Mitteis, *op. cit.*, 284–85, 289

18 Longnon, *La Formation de l'unité française* (Paris 1922) 37

19 Halphen, 'La place de la royauté dans le système féodal', *Revue historique*, CLXXII (1933), reprinted in Halphen, *A travers l'histoire du moyen âge* (Paris 1950)

20 Fustel de Coulanges, *op. cit.*, VI, 644

21 *Ibid.*, 649

22 Ganshof, *Féodalité*, 79, 81

23 Reynaud, *op. cit.*, 18

Six: Italian society from Charlemagne to Otto I

1 The genealogical details are assembled in Tellenbach, *Königtum und Stämme*, 44, 45, 54.

2 Lot, Pfisten and Ganshof, *Les destinées de l'empire*, I, 578

3 For the details, see S. Pivano, *Stato e chiesa da Berengario I ad Arduino* (Turin 1908)

4 D. Bullough, 'After Charlemagne. The Empire under the Ottonians', in *The Dark Ages*, ed. D. Talbot Rice (London/ New York 1965) 323

Seven: The rise of the German monarchy

1 Fichtenau, *Das karolingische Imperium*, 234–35

2 Tellenbach, *Die Entstehung des deutschen Reiches*, 136, 153–54

3 Tellenbach, *Königtum und Stämme*, 12

4 J.M. Thompson, *Feudal Germany* (Chicago 1928) 294; L. Reynaud, *Les Origines de l'influence française en Allemagne* (Paris 1913) 118

5 The situation is briefly summarized in G. Barraclough, *The Origins of Modern Germany* (Oxford/New York 1946) 19–22.

6 See below p. 128

7 C.W. Previté-Orton, *Outlines of Medieval History* (2nd ed., Cambridge 1924) 168

8 Bloch, *Société féodale*, II, 222–23; Reynaud, *op. cit.*, 140–41, 180

9 The best recent evaluation is that of H. Grundmann, *Betrachtungen zur Kaiserkrönung Ottos I* (Bayerische Akademie der Wissenschaften, phil.-hist. Klasse, Munich 1962, Heft 2).

Eight: The Anglo-Saxon achievement

1 F.M. Stenton, *Anglo-Saxon England* (Oxford 1943) 253

2 Mitteis, *Der Staat des hohen Mittelalters*, 159

3 See above, p. 98

4 The sources for early Anglo-Saxon government are few and difficult. The main text is the so-called Tribal Hidage, briefly discussed by Stenton, *Anglo-Saxon England*, 292–94. This document refers primarily to Mercia, but it is possible – as Jolliffe among others has shown – to piece together sufficient evidence to indicate that similar arrangements were in force in other regions from Northumbria to Kent, Surrey, Sussex and Cornwall. Neither the evidence nor the conclusions to which it points can be discussed in detail here.

5 R.H.C. Davis, 'Alfred the Great: Propaganda and Truth', *History*, LVI (1971), 169–82

6 See above, pp. 108, 116

7 Stenton, *op. cit.*, 407

8 Davis, *op. cit.* 178

9 Chadwick, *Studies on Anglo-Saxon Institutions* (Cambridge 1905) 207; the text is printed in A.J. Robertson, *Anglo-Saxon Charters* (Cambridge 1939) 246–49, and has been reconsidered by D. Hill in *Medieval Archaeology*, XIII (1969) 84–92.

10 Stenton, *op. cit.*, 262

11 Jolliffe, *Constitutional History*, 120

12 Stenton, *op. cit.* 290

13 Chadwick, *op. cit.*, 224–28

14 Jolliffe, *op. cit.*, 116–20; Stubbs, *Select Charters* (9th ed.) 79.

15 This view goes back to Round and Maitland, and was adopted with modifications by Stenton, *op. cit.*, 295, for whom 'in origin the hundred was a district assessed to public burdens at a round hundred hides'. See J.H. Round, *Feudal England*, (new ed. 1964).

16 Thus Lancashire – which did not, however, emerge as a separate county before the twelfth century – was poor and sparsely populated. It never, in spite of its size, had more than nine hundreds, and eventually only six. Earlier the six hundreds between the Ribble and Mersey (subsequently reduced to four) were attached to Cheshire, and the lands north of the Ribble were attached to Yorkshire. See the maps in the *Victoria History of the County of Lancaster*, I (1906) 268–69 and 290–91

17 Round, *Feudal England*, 86

18 Stenton, *op. cit.*, 295

19 Only 'a king strong enough to ignore local resentments' and 'indifferent to local traditions', Stenton writes (*ibid.*, 333), could have carried through a reorganization which so completely disregarded the ancient divisions of the land. No ruler was more likely to have

done this than Edward, who took military possession of the chief seat of the Mercian government and destroyed all that remained of Mercian independence. Thus, it seems 'probable that the artificial shires of the western midlands were created by him in the last years of his reign'.

20 F. L. Attenborough, *The Laws of the Earliest English Kings* (Cambridge 1922) 137; A. J. Robertson, *The Laws of the Kings of England from Edmund to Henry I* (Cambridge 1925) 17

21 It is conveniently summarized by H. R. Loyn, 'The imperial style of the tenth-century Anglo-Saxon kings', *History*, XL (1955) 111–15.

22 The standard account is in F. Liebermann, *The National Assembly in the Anglo-Saxon Period* (Halle 1913); see also T. J. Oleson, *The Witenagemot in the Reign of Edward the Confessor* (London 1955)

23 See below, p. 139

24 P. E. Schramm, *A History of the English Coronation* (Oxford 1937)

25 Stenton, *op. cit.*, 538

26 See above, pp. 90, 96; for the Anglo-Saxon oath see Stubbs, *Select Charters*, 78

27 Jolliffe, *Constitutional History*, 53–55

28 See above, pp. 133–34

29 Stubbs, *op. cit.*, 86

30 See above, pp. 59–60

31 See below p. 163. It is true, of course, that in England, where developments were cut short by the Norman Conquest in 1066, the ministerial class did not acquire the importance it later gained in Germany. But Marc Bloch, in his famous article 'Un problème d'histoire comparée: la ministerialité en France et en Allemagne', *Nouvelle revue historique de droit* (1928) 46–91, and Mitteis, *Der Staat des hohen Mittelalters*, 170, perhaps underestimate the similarities in the preceding century.

32 Jolliffe, *op. cit.*, 93

33 W. A. Morris, *The Constitutional History of England to 1216* (New York 1930), and *The Medieval English Sheriff* (Manchester 1927) 21

34 G. Barraclough, 'The Anglo-Saxon Writ', *History*, XXXIX (1954), 193–215

35 Stenton, *op. cit.*, 348

36 See above, p. 88

37 Stenton, *op. cit.*, 674

38 *Ibid.*, 340

Nine: The New Europe

1 See above, pp. 20, 78

2 E. Hoffmann, *Historische Zeitschrift*, CCXVIII (1974) 529

3 H. Pirenne, *Economic and Social History of Medieval Europe* (London/New York 1937) 24–25; and in greater detail, A. R. Lewis, *The Northern Seas. Shipping and Commerce in Northern Europe* (Princeton/Oxford 1957)

4 L. Halphen, 'Le conquête de la Méditerranée par les occidentaux aux XIe et XIIe siècles', *Mélanges d'histoire offerts à Henri Pirenne* (Brussels 1926) I, 175–80, reprinted in Halphen, *À travers l'histoire du moyen-âge* (Paris 1950) 337–42

5 Pirenne, *op. cit.*, 35

6 *Ibid.*, 76

7 Lot, *Études sur le règne de Hugues Capet*, 225

8 U. Berlière, *L'ordre monastique des origines au XIIᶜ siècle* (Paris 1921) 132; J. W. Thompson, *Feudal Germany*, 56

9 Berlière, *op. cit.*, 190

10 Thietmar, *Chron.* VII, 30

11 For a sketch of the history of the reform movement, see G. Barraclough, *The Medieval Papacy* (London/New York 1968) 65–67, on which this and the following paragraphs are based.

12 See above, p. 136

13 For the emergence of the idea of a single German nation, overriding the separate tribal divisions of the east Frankish lands, see E. Müller-Mertens, *Regnum Teutonicum* (Vienna 1970). Contrary to the views of earlier German historians, the idea of a German kingdom does not appear before the eleventh century, and is only fully accepted after 1125

14 Berlière, *op. cit.*, 196

15 Thompson, *Feudal Germany*, 75

16 A. Dufourcq, *L'avenir du Christianisme* (Paris 1904–14) V, 357

17 F. Dvornik, *The Making of Central and Eastern Europe* (London 1949) 9, 62

18 G. Barraclough, *The Origins of Modern Germany* (Oxford/New York 1946) 107

19 *Ibid.*, 84–91

20 *Ibid.*, 81–82

21 Berlière, *op. cit.*, 243

Bibliographical notes

Though different aspects are covered in national histories, in histories of the church and in the literature on feudalism, there are few books dealing specifically with the ninth and tenth centuries as a whole, and their place in European history. There is a good short account in A.R. Lewis, *Emerging Medieval Europe, A.D. 400–1000* (New York 1967), which covers Scandinavia, the Byzantine empire and Omayyad Spain as well as western Europe, and a lucid chapter by D. Bullough in *The Dark Ages*, ed. D. Talbot Rice (New York/London 1965). H. Zimmermann, *Das dunkle Jahrhundert* (Graz 1970), is concerned almost exclusively with empire and papacy, and pays scant attention to the underlying social, political and economic developments of the period. More useful, though sometimes a little dated, are parts I and II of H. Mitteis, *Der Staat des Mittelalters. Grundlinien einer vergleichenden Verfassungsgeschichte des Lehnzeitalters* (4th ed., Weimar 1953), though in certain respects his earlier work, *Lehnrecht und Staatsgewalt* (Weimar 1933), is to be preferred. Two books by P. Vaccari, *Dall'unità romana al particularismo giuridico del medio evo* (Pavia 1936), and *Studi sull'Europa precarolingia e carolingia* (Verona 1955), also attempt to place the period in historical perspective; but the outstanding book, even though it is in the form of disconnected essays, is T. Manteuffel (ed.), *L'Europe aux IXe–XIe siècles. Aux origines des états nationaux* (Warsaw 1968), which is particularly valuable for the emphasis it places on political and social developments in eastern and south-eastern Europe. These are also dealt with, more briefly, in the composite volume, *Eastern and Western Europe in the Middle Ages* (London/New York 1970), particularly Ch. III (by Karl Bosl) and Ch. V (by Alexander Gieysztor).

If the literature on the ninth century is sparse, that on the rise of the Frankish empire in the eighth century and on Charles the Great is voluminous. For the most part it is unnecessary to list or discuss it here. The results of recent research on the empire of Charlemagne are conveniently gathered together in a collective volume, *Zum Kaisertum Karls des Grossen*, ed. G. Wolf (Darmstadt 1972), but the classical account by K. Heldmann, *Das Kaisertum Karls des Grossen* (Weimar 1928), is still in many ways unsurpassed, even if some of its arguments are no longer tenable. The current interpretation of Carolingian history is best seen in H. Fichtenau, *Das karolingische Imperium* (Zürich 1949), of which *The Carolingian Empire* (Oxford 1957), is an abbreviated translation, and in two remarkable articles by F.L. Ganshof, 'L'échec de Charlemagne' (1947) and 'La fin du règne de Charlemagne. Une décomposition' (1948), now conveniently reprinted, with other important essays, in F.L. Ganshof, *The Carolingians and the Frankish Monarchy* (London/Ithaca 1971). H. von Schubert, *Geschichte der christlichen Kirche im Frühmittelalter* (Tübingen 1921), is excellent for both the Carolingian and the post-Carolingian periods, and the standard text by F. Lot, C. Pfister and F.L. Ganshof, *Les Destinées de l'empire en occident de 395 à 888* (2 vols, new edition, Paris 1940–41), part of the *Histoire générale*, ed. G. Glotz, still retains its value.

L. Halphen, *Charlemagne et l'empire carolingien* (Paris 1947), though reliable and judicious for the reign of Charles the Great, is particularly good for the period after his death in 814; and another book covering approximately the same period is J. Calmette, *L'Effondrement d'un empire et la naissance d'une Europe, IXe–Xe siècles* (Paris 1941). Among the older literature, N.D. Fustel de Coulanges, *Histoire des institutions politiques de l'ancienne France*, vol. VI: *Les transformations de la royauté pendant l'époque carolingienne* (Paris 1892), is still worth reference. Also illuminating for the course of events in the ninth century is J.W. Thompson, *The Dissolution of the Carolingian Fisc* (Berkeley/Cambridge 1935), and the period as a whole naturally figures large in the standard histories of European feudalism, particularly Marc Bloch, *La société féodale* (2 vols, Paris 1939–40), translated into English as *Feudal Society* (London/Chicago 1961), F.L. Ganshof, *Qu'est-ce que la féodalité?* (2nd ed., Neuchâtel 1947); Engl. transl., *Feudalism* (London/Toronto 1952), and J. Calmette, *Le monde féodal* (new ed., Paris 1951) and *La société féodale* (6th ed., Paris 1947). There is also much that is important, for this period and later, in J. Goebel, *Felony and Misdemeanor* (New York 1937), which is particularly good on the feudalization of the west Frankish state, and the same subject is dealt with (under a deceptive title) by L. Reynaud, *Les origines de l'influence française en Allemagne* (Paris 1913).

Probably the best general account of the rise of the French principalities is J. Dhondt, *Études sur la naissance des principautés territoriales en France* (Bruges 1948), and there is also valuable information in A. Longnon, *La formation de l'unité française* (Paris 1922), and in two more recent works by W. Keinast, *Studien über die französischen Volksstämme des Frühmittelalters* (Stuttgart 1968) and *Der Herzogstitel in Frankreich und Deutschland* (Munich 1968). For the east Frankish or German lands reference should be made to G. Tellenbach, *Die Entstehung des deutschen Reiches* (Munich 1943) and *Königtum und Stämme in der Werdezeit des deutschen Reiches* (Weimar 1939), but some of the essays in G. Barraclough (ed.), *Medieval Germany* (Oxford/New York 1938), notably that by P. Joachimsen, are still worth consulting, and there is a good account of the role of Saxony in tenth-century German history by Karl Jordan in *Historische Zeitschrift*, CCX (1970), 529–59.

By far the best available book in English on Italy is J.K. Hyde, *Society and Politics in Medieval Italy. The Evolution of the Civil Life, 1000–1350* (London 1973), but it is understandably brief on the period studied here, as is G. Luzzato, *An Economic History of Italy* (London/New York 1961). It should be supplemented by C.G. Mor, *L'età feudale* (Milan 1952), but perhaps the best account of developments between 888 and 962 is to be found in two older works: S. Pivano, *Stato e Chiesa da Berengario I ad Arduino* (Turin 1908), and A. Hofmeister, 'Markgrafen und Markgrafschafen im italienischen Königreich in der Zeit von Karl dem Grossen bis auf Otto den Grossen', *Mitteilungen des Instituts für österreichische Geschichtsforschung*, Ergänzungsband VII (1907), 215–435. The literature on the formation of the Italian city-states, largely in the period immediately following that dealt with here, is naturally extensive. The outstanding monograph is C. Violante, *La società milanese nell'età precomunale* (Bari 1953), but two seminal articles by G. Volpe, in his volume of essays *Medio evo italiano* (Florence 1923, reprinted 1961), retain their value. Also important are G. Fasoli, *Dalla 'civitas' al comune nell'italia settentrionale* (Bologna 1969), and an article by H. Keller, 'Die soziale und politische Verfassung Mailands in den Anfängen des kommunalen Lebens', *Historische Zeitschrift*, CCXI (1970), 34–64.

The standard work on English history in the period is F.M. Stenton, *Anglo-Saxon England* (Oxford/Toronto 1943, 3rd ed. 1971), to which more recent surveys, e.g. D.J.V. Fisher, *The Anglo-Saxon Age* (London 1973), add little. For all its merits, however, Stenton's book is a little noncommittal on controversial matters, and should be supplemented, where necessary, by reference to more specialized works, particularly on the legal, institutional and constitutional aspects. Here H.M. Chadwick, *Studies on Anglo-Saxon Institutions* (Cambridge 1905), a seminal work, is still basic. Reliable, also, is W.A. Morris, *The Constitutional History of England to 1216* (New York 1930); and J.E.A. Jolliffe, *The Constitutional History of Medieval England* (London 1937, 4th ed. 1961), if sometimes a little idiosyncratic, is always instructive and illuminating. The more specialized literature, so far as relevant, is referred to in the footnotes to Chapter VIII.

The beginnings of recovery in Europe after the Viking, Saracen and Magyar invasions, have been much discussed. Volumes I (*The Agrarian Life of the Middle Ages*) and II (*Trade and Industry in the Middle Ages*) of the *Cambridge Economic History of Europe* (Cambridge 1941 and 1952), are a useful source of information. In addition, for the revival of commerce, reference should be made to A.R. Lewis, *Naval Power and Trade in the Mediterranean, A.D. 500–1100* (Princeton/Oxford 1957), and *The Northern Seas. Shipping and Commerce in Northern Europe, A.D. 300–1100* (Princeton/Oxford 1958). The agricultural revival is discussed by R. Latouche, *The Birth of the Western Economy* (London/New York 1967), Marc Bloch, *Les caractères originaux de l'histoire rurale française* (Oslo 1931), Engl. transl., *French Rural History* (London/Berkeley 1967), and G. Duby, *The Early Growth of the European Economy* (London/Ithaca 1974), which may be supplemented by D. Herlihy, 'The Agrarian Reform in Southern France and Italy, 801–1150', *Speculum*, XXXIII (1958), 23–41, and for Germany, by P. Döllinger, *L'Evolution des classes rurales en Bavière* (Paris 1949). But the brief over-all account by H. Pirenne, *Economic and Social History of Medieval Europe* (London/New York 1937), is still clear and incisive, marked as it is by that penetrating insight into the general course of development for which its author was famous.

List of illustrations

Pentateuch and Joshua, 11th-
century English MS.
British Museum

50 Page from *Beowulf*; Anglo-Saxon
MS., *c.* 1000. Cotton MS. Vitellius
A. xv, fol. 132.
British Museum

51 Christ in Majesty, with group of
Bohemians; *De Civitate Dei* by
St Augustine, *c.* 1200. MS. A7,
fol. 1v.
St Vitus Chapter Library, Prague

52 King Stephen I in coronation robes;
initial from picture chronicle of
Marcus of Kalt, 14th century,
fol. 19d.
National Library, Budapest

53 Baptism of the Russians, *c.* 990;
Manasses Codex, 1345.
Biblioteca Apostolica Vaticana

54 Canute the Great and queen Emma
placing a cross on the altar of
Winchester Abbey; detail from
Liber Vitae, Winchester, 10th
century.
British Museum

55 Detail from St Gall plan of
monastery, showing (left) church
with infirmary and (right) cloister,
c. 816. Stiftsbibliothek, St Gallen

56 St Luke in ecstasy; gospels of
Otto III, 983/1002, cod. Lat. 4453,
fol. 139v.
Bayerische Staatsbibliothek

57 St Dunstan; detail from MS., 10th
century.
Bodleian Library, Oxford

58 Polish soldiers; detail from a silver
bowl, 11th century, Wloclawek.
Panstwowe Muzeum Archeoliczne,
Warsaw

59 Henry II holding a jewelled Gospel
book; MS. from Abbey Seeon,
11th-century MS. Bibl. 95, fol. 7v.
Staatsbibliothek Bamberg

60 Emperor Conrad II and his son
Henry III; stained-glass window,
12th century.
Strasbourg cathedral

61 Emperor Henry III between two
bishops; from Evangelium of
Henry III, *c.* 1040.
Staatsbibliothek Bremen

Index

Page numbers in italic refer to illustrations